Guns In America
Common Sense versus Nonsense

By Steve Freeman

Copyright 2013, Steve Freeman. All rights reserved. Printed in the United States of America. Except as permitted under the United States Copyright Act of 1976, no part of this publication may be reproduced or distributed in any form or by any means (electronic, mechanical, photocopy, recording, or otherwise) or stored in a database or retrieval system, without the prior written permission of the publisher or the author, except in the case of brief quotations embodied in critical articles and reviews.

For the victims… their families… and their friends.

CONTENTS

PREFACE

INTRODUCTION   1

PART 1   (Prior to Sandy Hook)   11

PART 2   The Unthinkable   33

APPENDIX A   How to Argue Gun Control   79

APPENDIX B   Stand Your Ground   90

APPENDIX C   23 Initiatives   94

Acknowledgements   97

PREFACE

This is a book for adults. It is not meant for kids.

Each year in America somewhere between 30-40% of all gun purchases are made without having to go through a background check. As year after year goes by, the number of guns purchased this way adds up. With over 300 million guns in possession in America, no one knows for sure (or even close) how many of these guns are in the hands of criminals, or people with mental illness, or people of ill-will, or people who may one day snap.

The primary purpose of this book isn't necessarily meant to scare people. Oh, bull… who's fooling who? This is a scary issue. Imagine some bad or crazy person in your own neighborhood who's armed with one or more guns, or assault weapons. Imagine someone bad or crazy targeting the next place you or your child might happen to be at… at the wrong time. Imagine being face to face with a gun, staring down its barrel. Imagine being a victim… or a friend or loved one being a victim. Imagine. Imagine. Just imagine. Try also to imagine what we can do about this.

Guns In America is an expanded version of a chapter from an earlier book- *Is America Stupid?* The former book is being re-written to include tales of the Tea Party successfully shutting down the government, as well as other silly and cynical adventures of both parties that have taken place since the 2012 elections. Sadly, however, the book's chapter on "Guns," has required an immediate re-write, since there is nothing more symbolic of the breakdown of our government- and the concept of *Democracy*- than the failure of there being no new gun laws enacted in the aftermath of the Sandy Hook Elementary School massacre.

The *framework* of the original chapter has been kept the same, because there is now a "before" and "after" to the gun debate… whatever was said *before* this horrible tragedy and whatever has been and is still being said *afterwards*. Some of the dialogue in the debate hasn't changed, but the images in people's minds are way different due to the deaths of twenty schoolchildren. Hopefully, there is never going to be another "after" to Sandy Hook. But who are we kidding? There may possibly be something even worse, even more horrendous… unless something is done.

Part I of this book, written prior to Sandy Hook, was written without the thought or notion of a massacre like this ever happening- which isn't entirely accurate. Most likely every adult or adolescent's mind- even some younger minds- have imagined something like Sandy Hook for a second or two or more. Especially with today's movies, television, video games and news events, imaginations are more inclined to go places that they didn't previously travel. Most of us think of, or worry about such tragic assaults out of fear and concern of other people's dark thoughts. That's why we fear certain people having weapons.

So, please keep in mind, the first part of the book- following the *Introduction*- may even sound a bit tempered compared to the anger and frustration that was unleashed by most Americans right after Sandy Hook. Immediately after this tragedy, both sides of the gun issue- those wanting more guns in America and less gun control *versus* those wanting less guns and more gun control- became fired up. The gloves flew off and both sides really went at it. And rightfully so. This is a major battle… since so many lives are at stake.

INTRODUCTION

A few days after the Sandy Hook Elementary School massacre, President Obama commissioned a task force chaired by Vice President Biden to come up with a plan to strengthen the nation's gun control laws. The goal of the task force was to better protect the innocent in our society and to try to prevent future massacres from happening. (Oh, and by the way, to cut down on *all* gun violence.)

The task force came up with 23 initiatives that were quickly narrowed down to *three* key provisions- *universal background checks, a ban on the civilian sale of assault weapons, and a 10 round limit on high capacity ammunition magazines.*

Two *Washington Post/ABC News Polls* taken after the Sandy Hook shooting, as well as various other polls, showed 91% of Americans to be in favor of universal background checks for gun purchases- meaning that every sale of a firearm would be subject to a criminal or mentally ill investigation. The polls also showed that 57% of Americans wanted to ban the civilian sale of all assault weapons as opposed to 41% who did not, and 65% supported limiting the bullet capacity in gun magazines to no more than 10.

Pretty good numbers for change- don't you think?

Not if you look at this as a game of poker- and the best and most skilled player at the table is, beyond dispute, the *National Rifle Association*. Here's how the NRA decided to play their hand... and easily win (or in this case, defeat) the entire pot that was on the table- background checks, assault weapons ban, and magazine limits:

First, concede to nothing! Even if you have no sane reason, nor any possible argument, whether coherent or not, to being opposed to 91% of the nation, make believe there *is* an argument. Say anything you want, no matter how bizarre, no matter how crazy; just look convinced- as if you know something that the other side doesn't know- that it's okay for anyone to purchase weapons without having to submit to *any* scrutiny whatsoever (through gun shows, the internet, or private sellers). And don't stop... do not stop showing how intense and impassioned you are about your dishonest and crazy beliefs. Eventually, your opponents won't even want to touch or go near the other two *less* overwhelmingly popular issues- assault weapons and magazines clips. On these two issues they will fold their hands faster than people fleeing a crowded mall if they were to hear a balloon pop.

Now, a lot of people may wonder: How can a strategy like this possibly work? How can you win with such nonsense? In fact, how is it even possible to fool the tiny 8% into agreeing with you (1% has no opinion) that background checks don't work, are useless... and worse yet, they're an inconvenience?

Easy. Very easy. First of all, you assume that not all Americans are very bright. (Give that some thought for a few seconds.) Next, you get other public voices- politicians, talk show hosts, and certain media outlets- to echo your nonsense 24 hours a day. Soon, not only will some of your supporters who woke up after the horrible tragedy at Sandy Hook with a change of heart, feeling that there *should* be stronger gun control... not only will they come crawling their way back to your side (and your leadership), but the fire and passion and on the other side will eventually fade, because... that's always been the case. That's just how it is... people have to get back to their lives. Not everyone can keep thinking about these sad tragedies day in and day out. That's understandable. And so... you win, NRA. Victory is yours. Time is always on *your* side. And therefore, nothing has changed. Still, any disturbed person, criminal or non-criminal, can easily attend a gun show, go on the internet, or hook up with a private seller... and purchase all the firearms they can afford, including assault weapons.

Therefore... Sandy Hook meant nothing.

3 | Guns In America

The debate over guns in America is a mind-numbing spectacle. To be sure, right after the Sandy Hook Elementary School massacre it looked almost for certain that something would finally get done about strengthening America's gun control laws. Even some politicians and public voices who had always been fiercely opposed to tighter gun control (mostly Republicans) were now agreeing that there had to be some changes. They were finally ready to make significant concessions. Instead, it became a *battle royale* to institute even one tiny little change (universal background checks). And for a reason that most Americans still aren't aware of, or simply don't understand, even though the United States Senate voted 54-46 *in favor* of instituting this tiny sensible change (that 91% of Americans were in favor of), the legislation- best known as the *Manchin-Toomey Bill*- went down to defeat.*

* * * * *

There is hardly a better example of a blueprint of America's severely damaged political system than the topic of gun control. This is where the whole system has decided to go *all* wrong *all* at once. It seems that nothing can instinctively or legislatively ever get done to simply even *try* to cut down on the number of mass shootings or the *tens of thousands* of other acts of gun violence that take place in America each

---

*In the U.S. Senate, any legislation (that's not budgetary) can be defeated if it does not get at least 60 out of the 100 possible Senate votes. Most people think a "democracy" means that a simple *majority* rules- anything over 50%. That's not the case in America- due to what is known as the "filibuster." A filibuster can actually make it so that the *minority* rules- since the minority can prevent almost any legislation from going through to the President to be signed into law. Got that, America? If the minority wants to, they can defeat just about any bill that doesn't achieve 60 votes.

and every year (or the *hundreds* that take place each day). Many Americans, including elected officials, for whatever reasons, may hardly even care at all about these tragedies that affect others. Or, at best, no more than a drop. They either can't, or don't want to, relate to other people's pain. Those who do feel other people's pain are usually left wondering what has happened to America. It didn't seem to quite be this way just a few decades ago. Now our schools and universities are headed towards becoming armed fortresses. No doubt that movie theaters, malls, possibly even every Starbucks and McDonalds will be quick to follow suit. A lot of us wonder: How did we get here? And now that we're here, how do we protect ourselves? How do we protect our children? Less guns? More guns? Keep it the same? What a fun debate to keep having. But 91%?! If you can't get something done with 91% support, then you have a problem- a real serious problem.

A lot of the fault with this issue lies on the shoulders of President Obama. It's truly mind-boggling how lacking he was on gun control during his first term in office. He would hardly touch the subject. And when asked during a Presidential debate (in Denver, Colorado, no less) about what should be done about the problem- just a few months after the Aurora, Colorado movie theater massacre- his response was so weak it seemed as if someone (the NRA?) was holding a gun to his head. The only thing worse was his opponent's response, which was even far more pathetic- that we don't *need* any new gun control laws. The President, though, did redeem himself after Sandy Hook- at least somewhat. He finally came alive on the issue. And on the day that the legislation went down to defeat by *winning* 54-46 (still confused?), the President gave possibly his most powerful and concise speech ever.

Naturally, he was angry. Oh, was he angry! He called the NRA *dishonest*- for spreading misleading facts about the bill- and chided the Senators who voted against the bill, questioning what their purpose was for them even being in the Senate. He chose some of the strongest words he ever spoke, which was about time, but he made one mistake (depending on who's scoring). He was very critical of the Senators who voted "no" on the bill, but he made a point of stating that they were "good people." Really? Are they? They had just kept it possible for the next mass murderer, or the next one, or the one after that… or some angry, gun-crazed maniac wanting to commit a single murder, to still easily get their hands on powerful killing machines. And these Senators who allowed that are good people? Tell that to the families of the next victims! (The President has got to define his definition of "good.")

(Note: Prior to this legislative vote on the Manchin-Toomey Bill, some of the families of the victims of Sandy Hook went to the nation's capitol and made the rounds of several Senators, trying to persuade them to vote "yes" on the bill. They shared their thoughts, their opinions, and related the horror of their experience to the Senators they met with. In an interview afterwards, the sister of one of the teachers who was gunned down while trying to protect her class said that most of the Senators she spoke to would just return a blank stare at her. She said she felt as if *"no one was there"* while she was speaking to them, and she got the impression they were going to vote *against* the bill no matter what she had to say to them. It just makes you wonder. It really, really, really makes you wonder.)

The corruption and shallow self-interests of politicians and businesses involved in preventing gun control legislation are two major reasons why there is a giant *wound* in America's soul. For many Americans, it feels like a heavy blow to the gut- especially after something like Sandy Hook- the inability to do something… anything… to stop these endless, heartbreaking tragedies from happening. Millions of people are just mystified and wonder why- why can't something be done? In fact, as far as this particular issue goes, it truly is *the People of the United States* versus *the National Rifle Association*, since, on a national level, the Republican and Democratic officials cancel each other out through their votes. The Republicans vote *against* gun control and the Democrats vote *for* it- minus less than a handful on either side. Therefore, *de facto,* it becomes "the People" who are *virtually* up, face to face, against the NRA, since the legislators are useless. And the face of the NRA is its Executive Vice President and spokesperson, Wayne LaPierre, who, although his title doesn't reflect it, by all appearance and means, seems to undoubtedly be the true leader of the NRA.

For years now, and especially after Sandy Hook, LaPierre has been the one everyone sees testifying before Congress and appearing at press and news conferences stating the NRA's platform and beliefs. And even though he had tried doing this after other previous shootings and massacres, for Sandy Hook, more than ever, LaPierre determinedly tried to re-direct the focus off of guns (as the problem for all these shootings) and onto people with mental illnesses- claiming that *"America doesn't have a problem with guns... America has a problem with its mentally ill."* And to a point he's right. The way we handle and treat our mentally ill leaves a lot to be desired. But not all horrific shootings are carried out by the mentally ill! Only around 5% of all gun homicides are committed by someone with a mental illness. And LaPierre knows that! In fact, later on in the book, we're going to explore some key questions about mental illness, as well as ask what could possibly be the most *important* key question of all- *Is LaPierre mentally ill?* Seriously... when you hear LaPierre talk or read some of the things that he says about gun control (and the people who favor it), you'll understand why this question has to be asked. LaPierre (and others) want to increase the number of guns in our society. That's not what makes him mentally ill- bloodthirsty and greedy perhaps, but not mentally ill. Or, maybe it does. (We'll have to get a Presidential definition on that, too.) LaPierre will get mentioned quite a bit in this book, since he *is* the face of the NRA.

It's obvious that one of the primary intentions of this book is to go after the false arguments put forward by the NRA (and other gun organizations). These arguments, along with skillful, yet simple slogans, help enable the NRA to keep finding ways to win and keep getting their way. Even though they have more people *disagreeing* with them than *agreeing*, and despite the absurdity of some of their arguments- some of which, they can't possibly believe in themselves- they keep winning. It can't just be the silly slogans, can it? There has to be more.

Steven Greenberg <u>www.greenberg-art.com</u>   *Reprinted with permission.*

Another major intention and purpose of this book is to show that there *are* solutions to the problem (despite what LaPierre says) of guns in our society. That seems to be the *great myth*- that there aren't any solutions. Strip away the politics, take away the voices that too many Americans take seriously- although, they don't take Americans the same way- and there *are* solutions.

For various reasons that will be laid out in the book, there doesn't seem to be *any* strong desire on the part of legislators to solve this problem. Now, some will naturally respond to that by saying that the government cannot- nor should it- be asked to solve every problem or issue. Others, however, would rather it be the government than the NRA or the gun industry, the ones many Americans feel are responsible for the problem. But realistically, everyone knows that won't happen. They know, for the most part, that today's legislators won't do much- or anything- and that's why several groups in favor of stronger and more responsible gun control have sprung up using social media to try and effect changes.

One thing this book is *not* going to do is go over the history of guns. There are plenty of books and other materials for that. Nor will it try to interpret the 2nd Amendment. (There will be a few unavoidable mentions- especially at the beginning, but not much more.) The Supreme Court has already had a few go-arounds with the 2nd Amendment and there is still no universal consensus as to what the Amendment's intended meaning truly is. Not even close. There is so much more to the gun debate then its history or an awkwardly worded sentence- although, it may not have sounded awkward in the 18th century. Nevertheless, the 2nd Amendment is still a big factor in the debate and is always there for gun advocates to fall back on when claiming (or defending) their *right* to possess firearms, including extremely powerful ones. These twenty-seven words have sparked many years of intense debate. And yet, if this amendment was never written at all, or was composed differently, the controversy over guns- every single type of firearm- would most likely still be as intense. In fact, take a look at these words…and see what *you* think this sentence actually means:

"A well regulated militia, being necessary to the security of a free state, the right of the people to keep and bear arms, shall not be infringed."

Any thoughts? What do you think? Is *"the right of the people to keep and bear arms"* only meant as part of a *"well regulated militia,"* or is it meant for everyone? If you have no answer, that's okay. Even the most intelligent legal scholar on the planet cannot find the right words to discount the Supreme Court's decision if it doesn't concur with his or hers on the meaning of this Amendment, except to say that the court is pathetically *political*- to which the winning side on the issue will simply dismiss such a charge with impunity.

This is one tough debate. It's a debate a lot of people have chosen not to take part in, that is… until Sandy Hook. And as time passes, even after Sandy Hook, the attention it should be getting is fading- with a lot of people giving up, thinking it's a waste of time and that the NRA is just too powerful and cannot be defeated. But it may not be a waste of time! It's a struggle, yes… but hopefully, not a waste of time, since any effort to reduce the amount of guns in our society and keep them out of certain people's hands, plus eliminate some powerful, over-the-top weapons, can pay off in one or several persons not leaving their families way too soon or having to be pushed around in a wheelchair for the rest of their lives.

The sad (or ugly) truth is that there is no developed nation on this planet that has the amount of gun violence *per capita* than America has. No developed nation is even close. The fact that this is the case, flies in the face of American *exceptionalism*. American exceptionalism cannot just mean the standard of living (for some) or having the world's most powerful military. Living your life peacefully and not getting shot has to be in there somewhere. Sending your child to school and having your child be safe has to be there, too. Doesn't it?

Americans have an enormous right to be angry that their voices weren't heard or listened to after Sandy Hook. A whole slew of lawmakers ignored 91% of the country! Are Americans going to let them get away with that?

Wait. Before everyone shouts, *"Yes,"* let's stop, think, hope, and consider that maybe this time they went too far… in not listening to all those who want to live in a safer America and who don't want to see themselves, or anyone else for that matter, getting shot or having to dodge bullets… while just trying to live their everyday lives.

PART I

"Guns don't kill people. People do!"

What the *heck* does that mean?

Once upon a time, President Bush (Junior) was arguing against the FISA laws- the *Federal Intelligence Surveillance Act*. He didn't want them getting in the way of some of the spying tactics his administration wanted to use. His argument was, *"The FISA laws were written 21 years ago… the world's a different place now."*

Oh, and the world isn't a different place now than it was some *two and a half centuries ago* when the Constitution was written? If there was any kind of justice, President Bush would've been hooked off the stage right then and there.

It is absolutely ridiculous when pro-gun advocates point to the 2nd Amendment as one of their arguments against gun control. The *Founding Fathers* had no idea that guns were ever going to be this powerful or have the capabilities they have today. If they somehow miraculously had known that, do you think they would have even written the amendment? Or, maybe expanded it? Maybe they would have written a completely opposite amendment. And do you think the Founding Fathers also had any idea how many angry and unstable people there would be living in 21st century America- including foreign terrorists- and how easy it would be for them to get their hands on guns today?

The gun issue, like no other, is the single most extreme issue that reveals the way in which so many Americans care only about themselves. It's sad, but true, many Americans do not care about all the people getting shot out there, just so long as they get to have their guns- for whatever reason. Are the reasons legitimate? It doesn't matter. They're all legitimate to gun owners, and that's all that matters, so long as they can keep pointing to the 2nd Amendment.

But Amendments can be changed, or new ones written (not a very easy thing to do). There never was really that great a need or push to change the 2nd Amendment, even in post-World War II years when the government was fully controlled by Democrats. There wasn't the level of violence that exists in this day and age. Some of the notable violence post-WWII *was* pretty intense, but it was usually aimed at a specific cause. (In fact, guess who wanted stronger gun control back in the 1960s and 70s? The NRA- and Republicans such as Ronald Reagan. It's true. They weren't particularly fond of seeing the *Black Panthers* armed.) Overall, the violence just wasn't as mindless and random as it seems to be today. It's sort of like the current financial system. In the past, there wasn't the level of greed and corruption that exists today. Therefore, there are now more calls for financial regulation. And there are certainly more calls now and pleas for stronger gun control- especially after Sandy Hook. Be that as it may, the 2nd Amendment has become *sacrosanct* and there probably is no changing it, ever, or at least for a long time.

The sacred and *inviolate* nature of the 2nd Amendment is without a doubt the *rock*- the main part of the foundation that the supremely powerful *National Rifle Association* has built its formidable house upon. This one single sentence has helped the NRA develop into an *almost* omnipotent force, to become the powerhouse that it is today in America's battle over guns.

Indeed, the NRA is one of the most successful lobbying groups in America. Maybe even the *most* successful. Their ability to coerce and pressure politicians into getting what they want is unmatched. When they need to, they can gather up the baddest *bad-asses* in the country and scare almost any elected official or anyone running for office into doing what they want, or at least not challenging them. You can't even debate the gun issue without considering the big gorilla in the room, because they are the game changer in all this.

And yet, despite its current success and strength, it's hard to believe, but people forget that back in the late 1980s and throughout the 90s the NRA wasn't doing so well and was just a fledgling organization. There were a spate of school shootings: Paducah, Kentucky- 3 dead, Jonesboro, Arkansas- 5 dead, topped off by Columbine, Colorado-13 dead. There were also other high-profile shootings- including more schools- that occurred around that time. People were outraged and wondered just how many of these shootings there had to be until something serious was done about gun control. Especially after the Columbine massacre, people were incredulous and couldn't believe how easy it was for two depraved, revenge seeking kids to obtain such a cache of weapons that were used. And more than ever before, Americans pointed their fingers and directed their anger at the NRA, and their unwavering stance *against* controlling the sale and use of guns.

After Columbine, polls clearly showed the majority of Americans wanted stronger gun control. Rallies were held all over the country. Some were led by wounded Columbine victims and parents of the deceased. There finally seemed to be some serious gun control momentum. Membership in the NRA was already in deep decline due to the group's absolutist approach to selling guns despite more shootings and massacres. Even Daddy Bush (President Bush Sr.) had quit the group a few years earlier. Incensed over the callous way the NRA acted in referencing Federal Agents in charge of enforcing gun laws as *"jack-booted thugs"* after the Oklahoma City bombing (in which some agents were killed), he withdrew his membership. Also during that period a movie was released, called *The American President*. In it, Michael Douglas, who played the President, declared the amount of guns in our society so dangerous that if he had to go door to door to rid the country of this problem, he would. Audiences in many theaters erupted in *cheers*.

The times, though... they have *a-changed*. They surely have *a-changed*. Could you imagine Daddy Bush giving up his NRA membership today- no matter how many shootings or how callous or insensitive the NRA chose to be? And how many people would cheer Michael Douglas' speech today? How many would have the guts to do so in public?

The NRA has re-surged. The NRA has won. How did it happen? A whole lotta love? No. *A whole lotta money!*

Although the NRA was founded way, way back in 1871 as a group to promote and improve marksmanship amongst the troops, and has grown since then to include sport and competition, training, certification, publishing, hunting advocacy and much, much more- for a long time now the group has primarily served as an *unofficial front* for the gun industry. The industry itself has always kept to the shadows and stayed hidden in the background. Just think, the thought of, *"How do they live with themselves?"* must be existential angst to these people (at least some would imagine).

The NRA has faithfully been the perfect surrogate for the gun industry- even willing to absorb all the bad publicity that comes from all the shootings. How they handle it is extremely vital to the industry's sales. In fact, as the NRA goes, so goes the gun industry. And despite a rough time for them in the 1980s and 90s, things began to change for the NRA- in a positive way- in the early 2000s.

After successfully getting George Bush (Jr.) elected President, the *politicos* who were responsible for that didn't waste time in letting it be known to all industries that felt challenged by limits and regulations, that they now had a really good friend in the White House. The White House doors were wide open to lobbyists. Some lobbyists visited the White House so many times, rumor has it they had chairs and sofas named for them. For the NRA, it was most likely a *thro*ne, since they were way much more than a lobbying group- they were a *political* group. It was as if someone in the White House had a nasty epiphany- that the NRA could affect the outcome of elections with a *corporate/grassroots* effort, since they already came equipped with still a huge membership and following. And by empowering their lobbyists with unfettered access all the way to the President's staff, as well as through the halls of Congress, it made the potential rewards- for everyone who had a stake- way too attractive to ignore.

With gun manufacturers (and their investors) pumping millions into the NRA, the group was, in a way, reborn. Success followed very easily- meaning they were now able to get just about whatever they wanted. It was all based on the same *simple* formula that was based on the same *simple* axiom that's been used throughout the ages between business and government: *First*, the NRA was able to hire the very best lobbyists on earth. *Second*, an enormous amount of money went into *hundreds* of politicians' coffers. And *third*, the gun manufacturers made record amounts of money each and every year.

Robert Ariail   *Reprinted with permission*

The NRA also had going for them a symbolic edge in the battle over gun control with the nomination of the famous actor, Charlton Heston (*Moses*), as their figurehead leader. Heston was President of the group from 1998-2003. At first, he was quite controversial in that some saw him as out of touch and questioned his thinking and motives- since in the 1960s, Heston was firmly on the side of stronger gun control. And now, here he was on the complete opposite side. It was odd watching him play the part. He even appeared pretty callous and out of step in coldly refusing to cancel huge NRA rallies that took place shortly after Columbine, as well as after the tragic shooting of a little girl in Flint, Michigan. Was that the Moses everyone knew? NRA members, however, didn't really care and saw him as a great choice to carry the group's banner. In 2000, after the embattled organization withstood the protests and their critics, plus aided by the passage of time, and buoyed by the prospect of a new, gun-friendly President in the White House, Heston re-captured the energy for them with a stirring speech in front of thousands. He stood at the podium, thrust a 19th century rifle up in the air, and referencing his famous line from the movie, *The Ten Commandments*, shouted, *"From my cold dead hands..."* The audience went wild... absolutely wild. They were once again emboldened, as that became their rallying cry. And months later, they got their main wish... as Bush *captured* the Oval Office.

The NRA has never had to look back since then. They've won! Whatever tough gun control laws there were, they have fallen by the wayside with the help of the Supreme Court and the Republican Party's *extremely* close ties to the NRA, plus, Congress allowing the Assault Weapons Ban to expire in 2004. It's now legal to carry a weapon outside your home in every state. In some states, they don't even have to be concealed. In fact, some states have even made it legal to bring a gun into a bar. A few drinks. A little impaired judgment. A dispute. A fight. Then... use your imagination. (2013 New Year's Eve- Sacramento, California- two revelers never did get a chance to ring in the New Year. They lost their lives in a bar over a spilled drink. Welcome to the *Wild West!*)

Gun control is clearly one of the most hotly debated issues in America today. Most of us have listened to, or been a part of, some wild and crazy discussions about guns. In fact, it's almost impossible to avoid coming into contact with people arguing about this issue, especially after a major shooting. But what is it, though... what is it that really drives the *intensity* of this debate? What makes some gun owners sound like they're ready to go to war over this issue?

To say, as it's often said, that it's mostly cultural or "genetically geographic" is a bit misleading. It's kind of true, but in a trumped up sense. It's just like when people say, *"America has a love affair with guns."* Yeah, some Americans do love their guns- they love movies with guns, they love the shooting gallery at the fair, and some love firing off the weapons they have. But *more* Americans have a love affair with staying alive and never getting shot or ever shooting anyone else. Guns might fascinate, but they also scare quite a few people. Western mankind has had a fascination with things that go *pop* ever since Marco Polo went to China and brought back gunpowder. (Actually, a few others brought it back before him.) *"A love affair with guns"* sounds poetic, but, in truth, it's just a small tiny percentage of the population that wants to go steady with guns. And even those people, left alone, they probably wouldn't care much about the debate- since *their* basic gun ownership isn't being threatened. However, the problem is that they are not left alone... because here, unfortunately, lies the story of today's America:

Not everyone, but many of those who consider themselves on the right- Republicans, Conservatives and/or Tea Party members- have a visceral hatred towards others who they identify with having a non-conservative ideology. And the bad blood and hatred wouldn't matter so much- it wouldn't be as rampant and intense- if it wasn't so successfully flamed by right-wing radio, television, and print. On the other side, Democrats and Liberals don't have as much hatred going on, but there is an intellectual dismissal of these extremists- whether it's deserved or not- that pours fire on this problem. With the gun issue being so partisan, it's frustrating to Liberals that people on the right take such a passionate position even though guns may not even be a part of some of their lives. But the hatred and passion gets lumped together with all other issues. And it all goes back to right-wing circus clowns whose interests are self-serving and profit-grabbing. Many on the right who are extremely vocal over this issue aren't stirred up with hatred by these clowns solely over guns, but by each and every issue.

It doesn't seem natural- the same people being overzealous on *all* the same issues *all* the time. No matter which party, it's just not natural. The odds of this always being the case are off the charts. So, the question is: Are you for or against something because you really care about it, or because you feel it's politically or socially incumbent upon you to feel the way you're told to feel? And again, to an extent, this is true for both parties. For, what does each issue have to do with each and every other *separate* issue. There is often *some* partial overlap, but usually not enough to completely wed each and every topic to one another. And yet, the Democrats and Republicans line up around 90% on the opposite side of each other on just about *all* major issues, even when it pertains to the ridiculous and the absurd- like, for instance, those who claim that the government is out to take their guns away from them. It may be that 100% of those who fear or claim this are Republicans, Conservatives or Tea Party Members. The opposite equivalent to this would be that most likely 100% of people seeking to levitate themselves in a large group through meditation would, for sure, be Democrats, Liberals or Green Party Members. (Oh, and by the way, the record for levitation, is still zero inches.)

The government has *never* given any indication of taking people's legally purchased guns away from them. It wouldn't be possible, and it wouldn't make sense. It would only leave criminals with guns. Is the government really going to team up with criminals? The idea is crazy, but that's what many gun owners on the right think! (According to a 2013 *Public Policy Poll*, 62% of Republicans actually believe this.)

Possibly one of the strangest discussions ever on guns may have taken place one evening on *The Chris Matthews Show* on *MSNBC*. Matthews had on as his guest, John Velleco, the Director of Federal Affairs for the *Gun Owners of America*. They were discussing a recent incident in Arizona where President Obama was holding a large rally in a campus gymnasium that held around 10,000 people. There were also other rallies going on outside the building, protesting one thing or another, and one of them included a man who was exercising his right to carry an exposed weapon. The man had been denied entry into the main venue where Obama was scheduled to speak and he wasn't very happy. Velleco was defending the man's right to carry his exposed weapon- regardless that he was freaking people out. He also argued that the man *should* be allowed inside the gymnasium with his weapon and he pointed out how safe it would be if *everyone* inside the venue had a gun, because, he claimed, they were all *law abiding citizens*.

First of all, how would he or anyone know that they were *all* law abiding? Were their foreheads stamped? Isn't it possible that some may not have been caught yet breaking some laws? And second, what if a law abiding citizen chooses that moment to stop being law abiding? There would not only be an assassinated President, but once one starts shooting, others will start shooting and before you know it... ten thousand people with guns firing away. Velleco then went on to say that he thinks people should be allowed to carry guns on airplanes.

This is how crazy it has gotten. This is Archie Bunker mentality. Fans of the tv show *All In The Family* may remember one of its funniest episodes ever, where Archie got to make a Public Service Announcement. A PSA was a 30-60 second spot on television that was popular during the 1960s and 70s where a citizen could express a counterpoint to that particular station's point of view. Archie's PSA was that everyone on a plane *should* have a gun, so that when the hijacker stood up and said, *"This is a hijacking,"* everyone else stands up with their gun and says, *"No it's not."*

Pretty funny, don't you think?

What was once funny and hilarious 40 years ago- a crazy idea from a silly (but kind-hearted) buffoon- is no longer funny. People are dead serious about this. One crazy politician who ran for Governor of Oklahoma in 2010 wanted to make owning a gun mandatory and he wanted to fine or penalize anyone who doesn't oblige. A few towns in America have *already* mandated that each home possess a firearm. Iowa has started issuing permits to blind people. Comedian Jimmy Fallon says that makes two groups very happy: the NRA and deer. The Missouri legislature is trying to approve the sale of machine guns to citizens. Hopefully, their Governor vetoes it- especially before they copy Iowa and approve it for blind people. Yes, it has become this crazy. But how... how did it get to be this crazy?!!!

Getting back to the previous issue of taking everyone's guns away from them- each and every day, not only are radio shows stoking gun owners' fear and paranoia that the government is secretly plotting to do this, but so are politicians, the NRA, other gun groups, gun magazines, gun websites, and certain media outlets irresponsibly doing the same thing. In Pittsburgh, Pennsylvania, there was a 22-year-old gun fanatic who was convinced that Obama was going to take away his guns, even though the President never made a mention or ever gave a hint of doing so. The man laid in wait in his home after his mother called the police on him and shot and killed 3 police officers. Almost the same exact incident happened near Fresno, California where a gun zealot ambushed a county sheriff and a police officer, killing them both. No one was coming to take away their guns, unless they purchased them illegally or stole them.

Is it possible that what should very well be a *non-issue* is clouding the minds of gun owners being able to see what is truly the *real* problem- that there are too many guns out there and too much gun violence?

Non-stop, we read or hear about shooting after shooting after shooting after shooting. Some even sound like fiction. But they're not.

They're real. The un-invited ex-husband shows up at Thanksgiving dinner and kills his ex-wife, her new boyfriend, her mother, his daughter, and his son. A father didn't like the ways his eggs were cooked, so he shoots his wife, his step-daughter and three others. A bitter ex-husband goes into a Southern California hair salon where his wife works and kills her and seven others. A six year old brings a gun to school and shoots the little girl sitting next to him. A 14-year-old boy shoots a 12-year-old boy because the 12-year-old seemed gay to him. (The 14-year-old had White Supremacist literature in his bedroom.) A 5-year-old shoots and kills his 2-year-old sister with his own rifle that was purchased for him from a company that uses a *cartoon cricket* to market their weapons to children. Two teenagers who weren't allowed entry to a house party return and spray bullets into the home, killing a recent high school graduate. A Connecticut home invasion by two armed ex-cons where they tied the father up, raped his wife and one of his daughters, and then strangled the mother and set fire to the house. Only the father survived. (There was no shooting, but would they have accomplished what they did without a gun?) In the town of San Bernardino, California, a wounded decorated Army soldier returns home after barely surviving an Iraqi suicide bomber that killed some of his fellow soldiers. During his homecoming party a guest got into an argument with his younger brother *over the score of a football game* and shot the soldier when he tried to intervene, paralyzing him. In Oakland, California a 26-year-old ex-convict killed 4 law enforcement officers in one day. In Amish country a crazy madman burst into a one-room schoolhouse and murdered 5 young girls. One reporter covering the story for a major network couldn't handle it and broke down on national tv. Can you blame him? And Virginia Tech- who can ever forget that? 32 people minding their business, trying to receive an education… gunned down. And there's more and more and more… times so much more.

It's sad and ironic that it has gotten so bad and so crazy with all the guns out there that it's hard to fault anyone who wants a gun for protection. But how big a gun?! And how many and how deadly the bullets? A 17-year-old shot a Congresswoman (Gabrielle Giffords) point blank in the head as she was having a *"Meet and Greet"* with her constituents outside a supermarket. Incredibly, she survived, but the crazed maniac managed to kill six others, including an 11-year-old girl whose neighbor took her to the event because she had shown an interest in politics. The gun he used had a 32-clip cartridge. It took him a matter of just seconds to commit his carnage.

Look, let's get real, gun owners… you've won! Gun opponents have conceded. They may not like it, but they've conceded. Americans *can* bear arms. But the concession is not because it is written in the Constitution, the concession is because it's crazy out there! You've made it crazy. Not exactly you, but the NRA, the gun industry, and bought off politicians have made it scary to go out at night… or go to shopping malls. (How many people have been gunned down in malls?) It would just be nice if there was some plan to make it less crazy. Is that possible? The gun industry wants to sell *more* guns. Some, as mentioned, want every adult armed. How did this concept of arming everyone ever arise? This was never heard of in recent memory. If the Founding Fathers wrote the Constitution with great reason, shouldn't reason be a dominant factor? Should the gun manufacturers be allowed to dump a *bazillion* guns into America each year? Shouldn't there be a limit? Should guns *ever* be sold to *anyone* without a background check? At the very least, shouldn't re-sales only have final approval by qualified officials? Shouldn't gun responsibility- locks and safe keep- include the heaviest of fines and penalties for loss or negligence? What's wrong with limits- limiting the amount of guns people can own?! They talk about the war on drugs, but do you ever hear any talk about the war on guns- *illegal guns?* What's wrong with a war on illegal guns? They want 25,000 more border patrol agents to keep illegal immigrants out. Can't they lend 5,000 of them to go after gun traffickers across the nation? (In the last decade only 38 new ATF officers have been added to the national total of 2338.) There doesn't seem to be too much of a desire for a war on illegal guns. Gun organizations pooh-pooh amnesty (gun buy-back) programs. That's ridiculous. They always get at least some guns turned in- usually dozens or hundreds. What about gun checkpoints? (Just like sobriety checkpoints.) How about making the penalties for illegal possession 2, 3, 4 or even 10 times more severe? You would think that someone facing a 10 year prison term for possession of a stolen firearm may be more willing to help track the dealers and thieves than if he or she was facing a 1 year sentence. Are there any decent answers to these questions or only dumb responses? Are these just dumb questions? Is this *sanity* or *insanity*?!!!

Here is the most common answer that gun control opponents give to any plea for sanity: *"Enforce the laws."* Enforce the laws???!!!!!! What they mean- actually, they don't know what they mean, but let's give them some help- is that if the laws were carried out then the wrong people wouldn't be able to get their hands on guns. Pretty intelligent, don't you think? You might as well hire a trillion policemen to be on every street in America at all hours of the day to eradicate jay-walking or spitting on the sidewalk, since, due to the insane amount of guns that are there, many *wrong people* have several ways to *easily* get their hands on guns. How can the laws be enforced on a *bazillion* guns that are out there? Where is the machine or crystal ball that can spot every illegal gun transaction? It's just not possible!

   Here is another common answer that gun control opponents give to any plea for sanity: *"You can't take away our freedoms."* What about people's freedoms to go see a movie? Or, to pray in a temple without getting killed (there have been numerous church shootings in recent years)? Or, to step out onto the streets… anywhere… at any time? Or, what about the most important freedom of all… the right to pursue happiness… *the right to live!?*

Gun advocates love their slogans. They love their nonsensical responses to gun control. They sound good. They may be completely empty in substance and meaning… but they work. Their followers love repeating them as if they're reciting scripture. The gun control side doesn't have many slogans, nor many words that can cut through to many a gun owner's heart… but they have statistics.

Here are some statistics:

An estimated 300 million guns are privately owned in America.

(No study is able to tell how many guns are illegally owned.)

Approximately 40-45% of all homes in America have at least one firearm.

In 2011, 5.5 million guns were manufactured in the United States for sale in the United States. Over 3 million guns were imported into the states.

In 2012, 19,592,303 background checks were submitted and processed through the National Instant Criminal Background Check System- *NICS*. 88,479 (.45%) were denied.

(Annual *gun sale* figures are impossible to assess, since a large amount of sales are re-sales and some are re-sales of the same *brand new gun* purchased that year. Plus, some background checks are for multiple purchases. But most of all, it's impossible to track private sales. Actual guesses range far and wide- between 15-30 million.)

In 2009, over 12 billion rounds of ammunition were purchased. The 2013 figure is believed to be a lot higher.

The annual cost to the government for gunshot wounds and deaths is $12 billion.

(Factoring in the societal cost of extended treatment, funerals, lost wages, insurance, legal fees, etc.- some economists consider today's overall cost to America's economy to be as high as $100 billion.)

In 2010, guns were responsible for 31,076 deaths. That's 85 per day. 3.5 each hour.

11,078 were homicides- 35%

19,392 were suicides- 62%.

(The risk of suicide increases dramatically in homes that have guns.)

606 were unintentional- 2%. The rest were police action or shootings deemed justifiable.

82 children under the age of five were killed by guns.

38% of all shootings- fatal and non-fatal- were of the ages 24 and under.

One New York City undercover operation found that 62% of private gun sales were to buyers who would not have passed a background check.

1% of gun-licensed dealers account for around 60% of all guns that are used for assaults and murders- meaning, they are involved in successful gun trafficking.

Gun Violence Against Women:

In 2010, 52% of female homicide victims killed by men were killed with a gun.

94% were killed by a man they knew.

Of those killed by men with a firearm, more than two-thirds were killed by their intimate partner.

Women who suffer domestic violence are eight times more likely to be killed if there is a firearm in the home.

Average number of handgun murders each year (suicides not included):

Japan- 19
England and Wales- 41
Australia- 45
Canada- 151
Germany- 269
United States- 11,078

---

*Gun statistics typically lag behind and are not usually current, due to cities, counties, states, and even nations that are none too eager to release gun data because of the effect the numbers can have on habitation and tourism. Plus, pressure from the gun industry has cut several agencies' budgets, making it more difficult to compile the latest numbers.

**Statistics compiled are from the FBI, the ATF, the CDC (Center for Disease Control and Prevention), Futures Without Violence, the Law Center to Prevent Gun Violence, the National Shooting Sports Foundation, and other sources. Some numbers are averaged out.

27 | Guns In America

Paul Berge — Reprinted with permission

"Guns don't kill people. People do." Yes, people kill people… but they kill them WITH GUNS!!

* * * * *

The Aurora, Colorado movie theater shooting…

LITTLE VERONICA NEVER HAD A CHANCE

Little 6-year-old Veronica Moser-Sullivan never had a chance to live a full life. She was gunned down in an Aurora, Colorado movie theater during a midnight showing of the newest Batman movie- *The Dark Knight Rises*. The shooter- a deranged, delusional and unhappy young maniac- 21-year-old James Eagan Holmes, entered the packed theater around 30 minutes into the movie. He had actually purchased a ticket and was seated in the first row at the start of the movie and then left the theater to gather his weapons (from his car that was parked near the exit door) and to put on protective gear. He left the front exit door wedged open so he could return. When he re-entered, audience members at first thought it was a harmless prank, since others were dressed up in costume for this special midnight premier. Holmes began his assault by setting off a couple of smoke canisters to create a diversion, which some thought was part of some special effects put on by the theater… and then he began shooting. He shot at the back of the theater first and then towards people running in the aisles. He wound up killing 12 people and injuring 58. It would have been more had not the 100 bullet high-capacity magazine he was using jammed.

In total, Holmes used 3 weapons to carry out his rampage: A 12-Gauge Shotgun, a Semi-Automatic AR-15- which is the one that jammed after forty-five rounds, and a Glock 22 forty-caliber handgun. Each weapon was legally purchased.

Although every shooting must in some way be *surreal*- perhaps this one more than most, since a movie itself is almost always surreal, especially a Batman movie. You can almost imagine the audience completely immersed in the moment, practically all breathing together as one… until horror walked in. (This act requires a deep sigh first, a really deep sigh, before even attempting to imagine why anyone in the world- save for some misguided terrorist- would go ahead and do this?)

By now, we've all seen photos of various mass murderers- *evil* or *insane*- with wry smiles on their faces. Some were taken right after they carried out their rampage and some were from earlier in their lives- and probably should have told us all that we may soon be seeing this person. Their expressions seem to be saying to us: *"Are you scared?... You should be."* Or, *"You'll never understand me...You'll never know what's inside my head!"* (Or, something similar.) And if they survived their assault and their picture was taken afterwards, it's almost like, *"I did it. I'm famous."* Or, *"Ha! I got you all!"* And again, *"You'll never understand me."*

Here's the problem: Even if the person *is* deemed to be insane, it's just extremely difficult for a lot of people to accept that *evil malice* didn't play a bigger part than the killer's *insanity*.

Therefore, let's say, in this case, that James Eagan Holmes thought he knew what he was doing and even rationalized his actions. There is no indication of that being the case, but what if he did? Just for the sake of imagining that Holmes had a mix of some normal and some disturbed thoughts, what differentiates Holmes from the millions of others who have violent thoughts going on inside their minds? (The answer, of course, is control- having control of your thoughts. But let's ignore that for a second.)

Almost anyone can have the destructive imagination to turn life upside down on its face. In this case- addressing Holmes- so what? You wrote your own script. It's not a difficult script to write. You practically mirrored the movie, or other action movies- which usually are a set of implausible, never-before-happened-in-real-life or never-will-happen-in-real-life scenes strung together to create a story. Sometimes a good story, sometimes dull and disappointing.

In this particular case- Holmes' attempt to turn fiction into reality- it was implausible in the sense that, once again, *"Why would anyone do this?"* This had never been done before, at least on American soil. In fact, Holmes even dyed his hair red to mirror *The Joker*- Batman's infamous foe. Did Holmes *really* identify with the Joker? Or was he just trying to one-up the character's creator for shock value? Who knows? Holmes may know. But he may be too much of an egotist to give away his secret. Holmes may very well have thought he had some genius inside his brain, plus a valid grudge against the rest of the *happy-go-lucky* world. He had neither. Was Holmes just crazy? Or, just plain stupid? Although, the real appropriate question might be: Who's crazier or who's *more* stupid- this mass murderer or a society that allows *any* egotistical psychopath easy access to powerful weapons and ammunition?

In the days following this terrible event, many people spoke about life being *"fragile"* and everything. After all… all you're doing is going to see a movie and you wind up dead. Does this prove how delicate and precious life is, since it can be cut short like this at any moment? Perhaps. But let's cut out the crap about how *"life is fragile"* or that all we can do now is just *pray* for Little Veronica and her loved ones. We wouldn't have to be praying for them and life would be less fragile if we had politicians (including Presidents) who cared more and had some courage about giving Little Veronica the chance to live a full and happy life.

This is what New York City Mayor Michael Bloomberg had to say after this shooting:

> *"You know, soothing words are nice, but maybe it's time that the two people* (Obama and Romney) *who want to be President … stand up and tell us what they are going to do about gun violence, because this is obviously a problem across the country… There are so many murders with guns everyday, it's just got to stop."*

Yes, it has to stop! There is no sensible reason in the world that makes it so simple for people who have ill designs- for whatever reasons- to easily get a hold of these powerful killing machines. Almost the entire country believes this. But the Democrats and President Obama have been bullied to no end by gun owners and the NRA. And the Republicans have been bribed to no end by the NRA and the gun industry.

What is going on with all these mass murders? (A *mass murder* being defined by the FBI as at least four deaths.) There have been slightly over 200 in the United States since 2006 alone (that includes all the well-known ones)... and yet nothing changes. What happened to all the serious gun control momentum we used to have? Where did it go? What happened to courageous family members who became powerful advocates after their loved ones became victims of gun-crazed shooters? What about the Brady Campaign, named after Ronald Reagan's press secretary, James Brady, who was shot along with Reagan during an assassination attempt on the President? They were once effective in getting gun laws passed. Where is their influence now? Are they all, sadly, just no match for the NRA, the gun industry and gun owners who hide behind their shallow slogans and shallow reasoning?

After the Virginia Tech shooting (32 dead) there was only a weak murmur about gun control. The same quiet response after the shooting of Congresswoman Giffords and some of her constituents. Where is the courage of politicians who truthfully care about the next victims? Where is the courage of politicians who truthfully care about Little Veronica and her now paralyzed mother who was also shot that evening and lost her unborn baby? Who will be next to join them? If politicians really truly care, they will make it much more difficult for there to be the next victim or victims.

Yes, life is fragile... because of cowardly politicians. Yes, life is fragile... because of bullies and greedy politicians who do not want gun control! It would have been nice if the 2nd Amendment had said we have the right to bear *popcorn* and go see a *movie*. Sounds silly, huh? Well it didn't say that someone had a right to purchase 6,000 rounds of ammunition over the *internet*, which is what James Holmes purchased just prior to his rampage. It would have sounded silly if the Founding Fathers had written that.

The silence after Aurora was deafening. It is unbelievable how little was said about gun control afterwards. Although, a few months later, when it was announced that the first presidential debate was going to be held in nearby Denver, it was gladly welcomed by those just craving for a major national discussion on gun control by the country's two prime political figures. Instead, the result was such a dud that millions of frustrated viewers probably switched to an episode of *Spongebob* for more wisdom and enlightenment. If this nearby tragedy couldn't get the two candidates to have a substantive debate about this issue, what would?

PART II

THE UNTHINKABLE

On December 14, 2012, Adam Lanza, a disturbed young adult with the usual characteristics- a loner, alienated, odd haircut, odd expression, odd dresser- he would spend lots of time playing violent video games, went on a murderous shooting rampage. He chose an elementary school... his old elementary school in Newtown, Connecticut, called *Sandy Hook*. No one knows exactly why he chose his old school. Perhaps he had a deep wound from his childhood that took place there. Perhaps it came up in his thinking that this was the most extreme horror he could think of. Perhaps his mind just snapped. Perhaps his thoughts were just *different*, and like other people with mental problems, difficult or impossible to understand. He had been diagnosed with *Asperger's Syndrome*, which is a mild form of *Autism*. Asperger's, however, is not related to violence. Full Autism, which is a brain disease that sometimes manifests in unpredictable behavior, *can* be related to violence, but usually not in a fully pre-meditated sense. The fact that he smashed his computer to destroy any evidence before carrying out his act, indicates some controlled thinking and planning of the massacre. Later on, it was discovered that he followed the events of other mass shootings. Still, this does not answer the question of why he did it. Therefore, let's forget the "why" he did it and focus on the "why" he *could* do it?

He was able to commit the massacre- 20 children and 6 adults- because he had access to six guns. The guns belonged to his mother and they were all legally purchased. He took along four of them on this day, and used two. One of them was a Semi-Automatic Bushmaster .226 caliber model XM15, similar to the AR-15 that James Holmes used in Aurora. He used this one to do all the killing. He was able to fire off 154 rounds in less than 5 minutes, using 30-round magazines. Some victims had 10 bullets in their bodies. Think of it, 10 bullets. There would have been more children killed if Lanza didn't have to change magazines several times. During one change, 11 kids were able to escape from a classroom.

A lot of people have wondered why Lanza's mother owned 6 guns. According to some who knew her, Mrs. Lanza had a survivalist outlook towards life- meaning, in this case, that the country (and the rest of the world) is *"going to hell in a hand basket"* and the police won't be around to protect you, so you better be armed and ready. She was not alone- thousands, maybe millions of Americans have this same outlook. That may or may not have been the reason for Mrs. Lanza owning 6 guns, but it's probably a good bet. She would practice with some of the firearms at a shooting range and take her son along with her so that he could learn how to shoot. Now, some might find it odd to introduce a young man with odd behavior and an already diagnosed mental condition (or disturbance) to these weapons, but maybe the mother thought it would possibly be good therapy and that she felt she had good control of the situation. Or, maybe... just maybe, the mother couldn't or was just unable to make a smart decision. Maybe she wasn't very bright. Perhaps she was overwhelmed by being a single mother with a mentally challenged son. It's not clear what her reasoning or lack of reasoning was.

The world, save for a few holdouts, now knows that it was a poor decision by the mother to have the guns in her home in the first place. Had Mrs. Lanza not had those weapons in her home, chances are 20 children and 6 adults would not have been gunned down just eleven days before Christmas at Sandy Hook Elementary School. The presence of the guns alone might have set off Lanza's imagination. No one knows. At the very least, she should have denied her son nothing less than one hundred percent complete access to the weapons. Instead, it appears she did just the opposite. It turns out the gun safe was in a really odd location- her son's bedroom. It's not clear and not known if Mrs. Lanza still tried to completely restrict access to the weapons. It doesn't seem likely and no one will ever know... because before taking off that morning to commit the massacre, Lanza shot and killed his mother while she still slept. And after the massacre... Lanza shot and killed himself.

Now, there won't be any describing of how Lanza carried out his murderous attack- how he got into the school and what he proceeded to do. And there won't be any attempt at describing the emotional devastation to the victims' families or to the rest of the school's children and their families. Almost everyone has seen and listened to the aftermath in terms of shock and horror, and sorrow, and has already pondered the tragedy over and over again in their minds. Many people still cannot stop thinking about it.

Within minutes of the massacre, as soon as people were able to comprehend what had just taken place, and that it wasn't some horrible dream they were having- the debate over guns in America sprang up quicker than it ever did before. It was like a collective, *"That's it. Something has to be done about these guns!"* It more or less came flying out of people's mouths- those wanting to say this for so long. In past tragedies it took a little while to come up, because wimpy politicians (Democrats) would get beaten down by accusations that by bringing up the issue of gun control after a murder or massacre they were exploiting the tragedy for self-purpose or political gain. This never made sense. What else was supposed to get them to bring up gun control, a friendly game of *Ping-Pong?* This just never made sense. Newly elected Republican Tea Party Senator Ted Cruz of Texas made the rounds of the media after Sandy Hook and used this tact as often as he could. Even after Sandy Hook?! Yes, even after Sandy Hook. You can say he had gall, but not one media person stood up to him. A *soft-approach* media and *cowardly* politicians had become protocol regarding this issue. In fact, it even became sort of weird that after several of these shootings over recent years, you would hardly hear more than a peep about gun control. Again, even after the Aurora tragedy, the little that was said about gun control was stunning. But now, finally, after wondering for so long about what it was going to take to finally get rid of these powerful and terrifying assault weapons, it seemed there was now an answer- the massacre of twenty 1st and 2nd graders and six adults charged with their care.

Would things finally change now? Everyone wondered. Was this the wake-up call for America? Most people- in fact, most of the world- felt it had to be. A lot of gun owners, including even some assault weapon owners who were shaken to the core by this tragedy, now seemed ready and willing to accept changes. But what would those changes be? The whole country was curious.

Being that the focus was on the type of weapon that Lanza used, most people instinctively felt there would be a compromise and they easily assumed what the compromise would most likely be. They assumed that since the majority of gun control advocates had already accepted the fact that Americans *should* be allowed to legally own and keep some *types* of guns, they knew they would probably have to accept that those who already owned assault weapons that they had legally purchased, could keep them. (Fighting against already purchased assault weapons would undoubtedly be long and futile.) But that's it! No more! No more *new* assault weapons! Even several Republican officials chimed in and agreed with that. But what about the NRA? What would the *big voice* in all this, the main lobbying force, the organization most responsible for legislating America's gun policies- what would *they* have to say about this tragedy and these weapons? Again, everyone was curious and wanted to know.

The NRA didn't comment. Seriously, they didn't say a word. They laid low for several days after the massacre- knowing that time would forgive them their silence- even though the whole world knew they were just buying time and strategizing their next move. They would only say that *eventually* they would have something to say. Therefore, there was plenty of guessing and speculation as to what it would be, with most of the country thinking they would finally concede to stronger gun control. They would have to. It only made sense. They were now so incredibly vilified that it seemed for certain they would finally give in to tighter and stricter regulations. There were even instant polls taken just a few days after the massacre that showed over 70% of NRA members were now in favor of banning assault weapons. It seemed to be just a matter of the nation hearing from the NRA itself exactly what changes they were going to propose and their ideas on how these changes should be carried out.

Finally... after seven days of silence, they held a press conference. And... of course... it was Wayne LaPierre, the *face* of the NRA, who spoke.

Let's cut right to the chase! LaPierre surprised, but didn't really shock the world in calling for not less guns and assault weapons in our society, but more! Seriously, he fooled everyone. He called for *less* restrictions, not more. He claimed that gun laws don't work- so, why bother. It wasn't all that shocking- surprising yes, but again, not that shocking- because LaPierre *always* advocated for more guns. "*If everyone has a gun, then the bad guys won't mess with ya,*" was LaPierre's usual reasoning. Even many of LaPierre's supporters were expecting something different this time. Instead, after setting up how dangerous the world is in the first part of his speech- and that we should all have guns to protect ourselves- LaPierre then went ahead and laid out a plan for America to protect our kids while they're at school.

His plan was to put a cop or an armed guard in each and every school. Yes... each and every school.

Wait! Wait! Wait! Wait just a second! *Are you serious?* You, NRA, you caused the problem- helping gun manufacturers pour 300 million guns into our population, including assault weapons- and now you want us to fix it... *your* way!? Again... *are you serious?!!!*

In the past, the NRA and other gun groups would always argue that schoolteachers should be armed. And that debate had already been taking place non-stop the entire first week following the massacre. (Never mind that teachers grew up wanting to be teachers... and not gunslingers.) But now LaPierre was addressing the nation with a slightly different plan, making the case for every school in America to become an armed campus.

Bruce Plante *Reprinted with permission.*

Here's the problem with making schools armed campuses: It doesn't reduce guns! For schools that have declared their campus a "gun free" zone, it adds a gun to a place where communities don't want there to be *any* gun at all! Many people who are able to think critically have come to realize that when there is a gun around, something bad is more likely to happen. Plus, it won't necessarily stop or prevent an attack. For those who don't know, there *was* an armed officer present at Columbine on that fateful day in 1999. It's impossible for one armed person to cover an entire school or campus- and a crazy or bad person may even be enticed by the challenge. Who knows? Don't you usually have to get by the armed security (good or bad) in most video games?

There are also two other problems with this idea- two major problems. The first one is: *Who is going to pay for this?!* It was right away estimated that it would cost over *$5 billion* a year to arm the nation's schools. Most NRA members are Republicans and/or Tea Party members. We thought they wanted to cut spending. Instead of spending $5 billion a year on a solution that may have only little or no effect, what about spending a fraction of that amount and doing everything possible to keep guns out of the hands of criminals and disturbed people?

And here's the other major problem: Not that the NRA and several other anti-gun control advocates really care- even though they always say they do- but what kind of statement does this make? What does this say about America? *"America, the greatest country on earth, needs guns to protect their kids while they're at school!"*

This probably wasn't the hopes and dreams of our Founding Fathers, our forebears, our parents, grandparents and whoever else. They most likely dreamed the opposite! And maybe if the NRA didn't help the gun manufacturers flood our nation with 300 million guns... we wouldn't be in this mess we're in today. Would we?

Some say we would. That's because gun groups and their supporters maintain there is *no* proof that reducing the number of guns in our society would exponentially reduce the amount of gun violence. But there actually *is* proof- England and Australia. Both countries have practically eliminated the availability of firearms and the amount of gun violence in both countries has plummeted. In Australia alone, it dropped 59%. And prior to their 1996 enactment of much stricter gun laws, after a shooter took the lives of 35 victims in the town of Port Arthur, there were 13 mass shootings in 18 years.

Since 1996, there have been zero. Yet America chooses to ignore this example. (It's as if math doesn't exist to some people.)

There was one major catch-phrase to come out of LaPierre's speech that evening. It went: *"The only way to stop a bad guy with a gun is with a good guy with a gun."* (The next day it seemed like every anti-gun control person in the country was repeating it.) Well, Mr. NRA... what if the bad or disturbed person didn't have a gun or couldn't get a gun? Without a gun, there would likely be no massacre. What say you, Mr. NRA?

(Note: There actually *were* protestors there during LaPierre's speech. And a few interrupted and challenged him. However, they were quickly hustled out of the room. He didn't respond to one of them. Nor, after his speech, did he take any questions from the press. He quickly left the podium.)

TONE-DEAF... OR SOMETHING WORSE?

Even though LaPierre's strange speech (or press conference?) was disappointing to most of the country, it didn't put the kibosh on the overwhelming majority of Americans' hopes for immediately strengthening the nation's gun laws. It was disappointing in the sense that human beings always have a warm hope and feeling that the other side of *any* issue will eventually come around and agree to work something out together that's for the betterment of mankind. Lo and behold, that didn't happen here. But it wasn't that worrisome, because LaPierre looked pretty weak and foolish walking away while journalists threw challenging questions at him. And plus, the overall resolve of wanting to prevent a tragedy like this from ever happening again was still fresh in the nation's heart- and many people thought that *nothing* could stop the momentum of this simple rationale.

But, as days began to pass, it did start to get a little disconcerting as some politicians began withdrawing their immediate reactions to sensible gun control. Was it because the NRA successfully got to them? In fact, they almost all delivered the same talking point as an excuse: *"Let's not make any rash emotional decisions while the country is still suffering,"* which is another way of telling everyone to just ride this out until the public loses interest. On the opposite end of that, the strength of the pro-gun control side lies in people *never* losing interest or forgetting what almost everyone felt crystal clear about in their gut after Sandy Hook. And that is, besides never wanting something like this to ever happen again, they felt for sure that something had to be done about these assault weapons and their availability.

Now, *talking points* are an effective and useful tool. And they are obviously aimed at the feeble-minded and only have to contain the tiniest iota of possible truth in them. That's why a whole bunch of them were released by the NRA and other gun lobbyists for politicians, talk show hosts, media outlets and others to use in the days and weeks that followed Sandy Hook to deal with the backlash against weak gun laws. So when people hear, *"No gun law would have stopped Adam Lanza from committing this rampage"* (not even close to being completely true), some think, *"Hey, yeah. That's right,"* and then leave it at that. But others who can think further, realize that's not the point and it's irrelevant. They happen to have this notion that if the bad or crazy person can't get a gun, and definitely can't get an assault weapon, and definitely can't fire more than 10 bullets at a time without changing magazines, plus other restrictions, then the chances of something this painful happening again are extremely thin. How does the NRA get their die-hard followers to not even think this? How do they get their followers to not question them on *anything* they say?

Here's another example:

One of the most frequent arguments of the NRA as to why gun laws don't work is: *"You cannot stop a bad person from getting a gun if they are seriously determined to cause harm."* Really? Is that true? Don't people often give up when something is difficult? Don't most people almost always give up or not even try certain things when they know it's close to impossible?

In fact, let's take a look at how people purchase or get their hands on guns... because this is what it's all about. Right? And whether you think it's the person that's the problem or the gun that's the problem, they have to somehow meet. Correct? So, let's take a look:

In order to purchase a firearm from a licensed store or licensed gun dealer a person must first submit to a background check through the *National Instant Criminal Background Check System-* or NICS. They have to fill out a form and answer a series of questions that looks for any criminal record or history of mental illness or dishonorable discharge from the military, plus other barring criteria, that prevents that person from owning a firearm. To *avoid* a background check, someone wanting to "legally" buy a firearm would either have to attend a gun show or find a private seller, where they don't have to submit to any check (except for certain states that have passed stricter gun laws than federal laws). This is known as the gun show or private seller "loophole."

(Note: There are 10 states, plus Washington, D.C., that require a waiting period for the purchase of some or all guns. A few additional states require a license or permit to purchase a firearm- which also creates a waiting period. The obvious rationale for this is so that someone in a *fit of anger* or *rage* cannot just walk into a gun store and walk out with a gun that same day, or for a few days. Hopefully, this gives them some time to calm down.)

The other ways for someone to get their hands on a firearm are to steal one, have someone else purchase it for you (a *straw purchase*), inherit one, receive one as a gift, or buy a stolen one from an illegal trafficker or dealer- something that may be easy for some, not so easy for others (depending on who one associates with). So, except for stealing or buying a stolen weapon, and even getting someone to purchase a weapon *for* you, it is pretty *simple* to obtain a firearm even if you can't pass a background check- since most states *haven't* adopted stricter laws than federal. Requiring *every state* to have universal background checks, meaning- gun stores, gun dealers, gun shows, private sellers, the internet, and when someone inherits or is gifted a firearm- would therefore make it *not so simple* for a criminal or mentally ill person to purchase a gun or assault weapon.

Representative Mike Thompson (D-California) asks:

> *"Why in the world would anyone not agree that you should get a background check before you buy a firearm?... If you disagree with background checks the logical jump is that you believe that it is okay for criminals and the mentally ill to buy guns."*

Yes! Exactly! Who, or what kind of person, would want to make it easy for a criminal or disturbed person to get a gun? Possibly another disturbed person?

A few weeks after his post-Sandy Hook press conference, in which most critics accused him of being *tone-deaf* and not hearing what 91% of the American people want, LaPierre went ahead and testified in front of Congress. He claimed that universal background checks don't work, because criminals would avoid submitting to them.

First, Senator Patrick Leahy (D- Vermont), who was addressing him at the time, couldn't make his way through this flawed logic (some Senators maybe ought to think of retiring), but then Senator Frank Durbin (D- Illinois) informed LaPierre that what he just claimed was *exactly the point!* With universal background checks, if they don't submit to the check, they cannot purchase a firearm- legally!

What was LaPierre's response to that? He claimed to not understand the point that Durbin was making- which is a typical practice for people who rely on a *following*. If you claim not to understand something- no matter how simple- neither will your following, since they can only be as smart as you.

The point is that by eliminating *all* major *legal* avenues of obtaining firearms without a background check- it is no longer simple for a criminal or someone deemed mentally ill to get a firearm!

This ain't complicated! It just ain't!!!

Acting ignorant, as if he doesn't understand a simple point, is not entirely what makes LaPierre a *disturbed* person. He may be shrewd or a pathological liar, as well as plenty of other *bad* traits, but there's other evidence that points to questions about his mental health. LaPierre seems to have an obsession with the mentally ill. And his obsession with the mentally ill may not always be for political or personal (economic) reasons. There may possibly be some deeper meaning to it. As mentioned earlier, from the very first words out of his mouth after Sandy Hook to subsequent crazy remarks, LaPierre was fiercely determined to shift the focus off of guns (as a danger to people's safety) and onto the mentally ill. Sure, he had done this before, but since Sandy Hook stirred up a ton of anger towards the NRA and their stance towards gun control, LaPierre was more desperate than ever to pull out the mental illness card. And in this case he had an advantage- a running head start- since it became known very shortly after the shooting that Lanza had been diagnosed with Asperger's. So when LaPierre says, *"We don't have a problem with guns in America, we have a problem with the mentally ill,"* he's stating something that's half-true and half-false. But all that really matters to his people is the part that is half-true- the part about the mentally ill. It's true we have a problem with some who are mentally ill, but it's *also* true we have a problem with guns! LaPierre wants the country to believe that it's just the mentally ill who are dangerous and murdering people, when according to various studies, only between 3-10% of all fatal gun crimes are committed by the mentally ill. (The figure is closer to 10% when drugs and alcohol are involved.) And yet, a few weeks later, as he was still saying this, a former Los Angeles police officer went on a murderous rampage of hate and revenge against other police officers and those he felt were responsible for getting him kicked off the force. The entire country became riveted to the manhunt for this former officer, Christopher Dorner, who managed to kill 4 people, including a police officer and a deputy sheriff, and wound 3 others, before committing suicide during a shootout with police. Dorner was not *certifiably* mentally ill. He was most likely just as delusional as the very next "delusional" person who feels that others are responsible for their problems. He was angry over his dismissal from the LAPD. He had guns to go along with his anger. That was his mix- *anger* and *guns*. It's not a good mix- just like *mental illness* and *guns* are not a good mix. And LaPierre's attempt to fool others into believing that just keeping guns away from the mentally ill is all we have to do, is nothing more than a pathetic diversion away from gun control.

LaPierre wants there to be a universal registry for the mentally ill. And there is nothing entirely wrong with that. There are issues with privacy and civil liberties that go in the opposite direction of LaPierre's opposition to a gun registry- but this can possibly be worked out, just as a gun registry may one day be satisfactory to gun owners as a way to solve crimes and for nothing else. But... how do we *know* if someone is mentally ill?! What exactly determines if a person is mentally ill? In some, it's obvious. In many others, it's not so obvious. Doctors and scientists have for years been trying to figure out standards and diagnoses for mental illness. Several leading professionals, including the current head of the National Institute of Mental Health, are at odds against the *Diagnostic Statistical Manual*- or DSM- which is considered the *Bible* of mental disorders. Throughout the ages, *genius* has been mistaken for mental illness- as well as depression, shyness, nervousness, religion, atheism, dis-obeying rules, challenging authority, rooting for the underdog all the time- plus many other types of human behavior. Determining that someone is mentally ill is not a simple process. There is of the utmost importance the issue of accuracy- getting it right. Even the very best psychiatrists and therapists can sometimes get it wrong. But even if someone *was* adjudicated to be mentally ill, still, all they would have to do, thanks to LaPierre and friends, is disguise their illness (if they can), walk into a gun show- or hook up with a private seller- and purchase whatever they want.

Bruce Plante *Reprinted with permission*

It's pretty scary, but some licensed dealers will, without hesitation, sell a firearm to a person who they suspect might have some kind of mental problem, but no actual record. Jared Loughner, the person who shot Gabrielle Giffords point blank in the head, purchased his weapon legally at a gun store even though someone who worked there allegedly knew him and knew him to be "strange."

But what about LaPierre? What about a person who will say or do anything to ensure that there are few or no obstacles for manufacturers to sell their weapons? Is *he* strange? Many people think so. Many people are torn between thinking that he's either evil or strange. He says he doesn't want the mentally ill to have weapons. Yet he's the one most responsible for them having the opportunity to easily get them! He is dishonest right to America's face and seems to suffer no embarrassment even when proved wrong. Is it thick skin or some *insane* evil persona? He is obviously out of touch with 91% of the country. So, you have to ask: Is he a *sociopath*? A *psychopath*? Just listen to some of his rants:

> "Our freedom is at risk in this (2012) election." "Without that freedom, we really aren't free at all." "They're coming after us with a vengeance to destroy us… to destroy us and every ounce of our freedom." "There's nothing the President will not do to destroy our 2nd Amendment." "When it comes to defending the 2nd Amendment we will never sacrifice our freedom…We will never surrender our guns. Never!"

Whoa there, cowboy! Whoa! No one… absolutely no one has asked you to surrender your guns. No one! Never!

What kind of raving *madman* does America have setting its gun policy?! Is he some sort of super-villain? LaPierre knows quite well what these words do to his millions of gun-toting followers. He knows these words- especially the key buzzword, *"freedom"*- gets them riled up. He knows this is promoting insurrection. He knows violence will come out of this, especially if gun control advocates start to achieve something. Gun control advocates are promoting the mildest of changes and yet this *madman* wants war.

And if he's not a *madman*, nor a *socio* or *psychopath*... but if his words indicate anything... then, in that case, for sure we're looking at a *paranoid schizophrenic*. Like when he imagines:

> "After Hurricane Sandy, we saw the hellish world that the gun prohibitionists see as their utopia. Looters ran wild in South Brooklyn. There was no food, water or electricity. And if you wanted to walk several miles to get supplies, you better get back before dark, or you might not get home at all."

This is exactly *why* we have to question LaPierre's mental state. Because, what's the difference of a certifiably mentally ill person warning everyone that *Plutonians* have arrived on earth and have taken over our planet (or, at least Congress)... and pro-gun control advocates wanting to see a *"hellish world"*? Nothing! There is no difference! Neither one exists! (Although, it might be the case that *Plutonians* have indeed taken over Congress.) And who wants to see looters running wild? People in prison, perhaps?

It's hard to imagine such a shadowy industry as the gun manufacturers having a better spokesperson than LaPierre. The man only *emits*. Nothing gets through to him. Once, while being interviewed by Megyn Kelly on *Fox News* after Sandy Hook, LaPierre was claiming that limiting the bullet capacity for magazines would *not* have affected Sandy Hook nor any of the other mass shootings that took place in recent years. When Kelly pointed out that while Adam Lanza had to switch magazines 11 kids were able to escape, LaPierre just completely ignored her. He just didn't respond and Kelly didn't press him at all. In fact, when Jared Loughner had to change magazines during the shooting of Gabrielle Giffords and her constituents, that's when he was tackled to the ground by a brave 63-year-old woman. Otherwise, there would have been more people killed. La Pierre knows this stuff, but he also knows he can get away with not addressing it. He can just sit there stone-faced and make believe the question was never asked or the point ever raised. It takes something extremely unique that most people don't have- being proved totally wrong and able to act like the truth doesn't exist or doesn't matter. Only *his* reality counts... and that's to sell more guns... even though they are being used to wreck incredible havoc. Most people this detached from the rest of the world's reality are often considered mentally ill. That's why if the question isn't asked today, it will most likely be asked in the future.

Kate Palmer   LaPierre: Blood on his hands   Reprinted with permission

Unfortunately, LaPierre is not the only public figure out there spouting nonsense about gun control. He is not the only one causing confusion, denying simple answers, and turning arguments upside down over the issue. He has plenty of company. Just a few days after the Sandy Hook massacre a caller phoned in to Rush Limbaugh's radio show to express his anger towards Lanza's mother (for allowing her disturbed son access to the guns). Limbaugh responded by defending the mother. Seriously, he defended her. He told the caller that he didn't understand the caller's *"animus"* towards the mother- since the mother had a legal right to the guns. What?! Twenty 1st and 2nd graders are dead because the mother introduced killing machines into her disturbed son's life and that's okay?!

When Limbaugh says something like this you really have to wonder whether he has a personal connection to the gun industry or whether he simply feels no upset about this tragedy at all, and to him, politics trumps everything. The politics of gun ownership is all that matters to him. A few months later Limbaugh even tried making a case to his listeners that the American people were overwhelmingly against background checks and banning assault weapons, plus the limiting of high capacity magazines. Seriously. Despite all the polls and information out there, that's what he tried getting them to believe. You have to wonder. You just really, really, really have to wonder.

These two, LaPierre and Limbaugh, must be soul mates. They are cut from the same cloth. Limbaugh teaches stupidity and LaPierre only makes sense to the very stupid. And speaking of the very stupid… the *incredibly* stupid… it gets even worse (if that's even remotely possible).

Most likely a high percentage of the country doesn't know who Louie Gohmert is. He is a Republican Senator from Texas. He may be the leading nutcase in the Senate. (Although, there are some others who give him a pretty close run for the money.) This is what Senator Louie had to say about the idea of placing limits on high capacity magazines:

> "... well, once you make it ten, then why would you draw the line at ten? What's wrong with nine? Or eleven? And the problem is once you draw that limit it's kind of like marriage when you say it's not a man and a woman anymore. Then why not have three men and one woman, or four women and one man, or why not somebody has a love for an animal? There is no clear place to draw the line once you eliminate the traditional marriage. And it's the same once you start putting limits on what guns can be used...then it's just really easy to have laws that make them all illegal."

What in the world is this guy saying? Comparing gun control to gay marriage to polygamy to bestiality????? How does someone start at gun control and connect the dots to marrying your pet or some animal you may have had a one night stand with? (And by the way, if Gohmert wants to marry his cat, dog or whatever other animal, please, no one stop him.) This Senator is not only strange- seriously, he's way strange- he's also complete proof that given the right circumstances, almost anyone can get elected to Congress... including this guy...

Ted Cruz- the already mentioned "other" Republican Senator from Texas. Cruz has become famous for almost single-handedly shutting down most of the government for the purpose of trying to prevent millions of people from getting health care. Cruz's whole trick is to use his *brainy* credentials (Harvard and Princeton) in a way that allows him to say (and do) the dumbest things... and get away with it. Here is what Cruz actually said while making the rounds of the media after Sandy Hook:

> "It is saddening to see the President... try to take advantage of this tragic murder to promote an agenda that will do nothing to

stop violent crime, but will undermine the constitutional rights of all law-abiding Americans... In any conversation about how to prevent future tragedies such as Sandy Hook, our focus should be on stopping criminals from obtaining guns."

What did you just say?! Can you repeat that, please?

What do you mean *"... our focus should be on stopping criminals from obtaining guns"*? Everything you say, do and vote for is aimed at *not* stopping criminals from obtaining guns! Don't you think some of us notice? And, what do you mean *"take advantage of this tragic murder"* (they usually say *"exploit"*)? What is the President supposed to use as an example of why we should have stronger gun laws, if not for the tragic shooting itself? This *"tragic murder"* is the *reason* the President is pleading for gun control... the *reason* the words coming out of his mouth are so emotional and ring true to most of the country!... Is this the best ya got? Are you serious?

This has been the sad strategy of the NRA and the anti-gun control lobby for years. They know if the issue isn't raised right away, it's never going to be. How low... and how shallow. And yet it has successfully caught on. It has successfully worked. The Democrats usually shrink once it's brought up. As Connecticut Democratic Governor Dannel Malloy points out, *"These Democrats* (in Congress) *are not exactly profiles in courage."*

Another Senator who uses this tactic is Rand Paul (R- Kentucky). Only, Paul phrases it differently:

"When I see the fathers and the mothers and them testifying... and I know they're coming voluntarily, and they want to come and be part of this debate... but it still saddens me just to see them. And I think that in some cases the President has used them as props... and that disappoints me."

These words- especially *"props"*- happened to get the President pretty mad and incensed. And rightfully so. Haven't these families suffered enough and earned the right at least not to be described as *"props"*? And haven't they sadly earned the right to show the nation the heartbreak and suffering that gun violence brings to a family, so that in the future it may only happen as little as possible or maybe even never? You would think this would be considered pretty brave of them that, despite all their suffering, they can even stand up and make this effort to honor their loved ones and try and make it so others might never have to go through what they're going through. And there is no bigger stage than alongside the President, is there? Plus, they're not being forced to do it, are they? Is Paul serious? He tries to explain:

> *"I'm someone who is presenting a face to the public... and the face I want to present is that I do care about those kids, and that I understand the grief that they're going through, and that I do care about it. Politics isn't only about facts, it is about whether you're seen as empathetic. And I do want people to know that I do care about those families and I understand their grief."*

No, you don't. If you really understood and cared, you wouldn't have said what you said- and you wouldn't have called them *"props."* Or, would you?

Paul and Cruz are true "darlings" of the *Tea Party*. The Tea Party pretends it wants to be known for fiscal savings, and yet, gun violence, according to a 2012 study by the *Pacific Institute for Research and Evaluation,* costs the government in tax money around *$12 billion* a year. However, when you add up *all* the costs- treatment, aftercare, funerals, loss of work, and other additional extenuating factors, the overall cost is thought to be as high as $100 billion each year.

Now, Paul and Cruz can claim that further gun control laws won't do *anything* to reduce gun violence, but why won't these "constitutionalists" (as they consider themselves to be) let the people decide on that? Instead, Paul, Cruz, and Senator Mike Lee (R- Utah) sent a letter to Senate Majority Leader Harry Reid (D-Nevada) declaring that they would filibuster, and not even let reach the floor of the Senate for discussion, *"any legislation that will serve as a vehicle for any additional gun restrictions."* No matter how many lives might get saved by *"any"* measure proposed, they declared they would be against it. And, not surprisingly, that was okay for many of their supporters. Again, it makes you wonder. It just really makes you wonder.

This brings us to another Tea Party favorite: Senator Marco Rubio (R- Florida), who others - including himself- are seriously envisioning being the next or one day future President of the United States.

Rubio doesn't have the *intellectual dishonesty* skills of a Cruz or a Paul- although, he'll eventually get there. (Paul once tried to explain why he thinks businesses should have the right to not serve certain races of people if they don't wish to. Cruz wants to abolish the IRS.) Rubio is a moron through and through. He goes on television arguing against the background checks bill, and threatening to also filibuster it, without having read the bill. When asked by *CNN's* Erin Burnett why he is against it, Rubio simply says that background checks don't work. Burnett doesn't ask why or make any attempt to get Rubio to explain himself, she just moves on to another subject. However, on *Meet the Press*, Rubio found himself cornered and was more or less forced to explain why he's against making universal background checks a law… (and it's a doozy).

> *"My skepticism about gun laws is that criminals don't follow the law. They don't care what the law is. You can pass any law you want, criminals will ignore it."*

Good point! In fact, why have any laws? Criminals are just going to ignore them. A law against robbing a bank- that's not going to stop a criminal. Drunk driving- that won't stop a drunk. Why have a drunk driving law? Beating your spouse or girlfriend- a law isn't going to stop someone in a rage. Rubio is obviously on to something. And when interviewed by Chris Wallace on *Fox News*, Rubio suggests that we shouldn't even be focusing on guns. His reasoning:

> *"We're focusing so much on guns. We should be focused on violence. Violence is the problem. Guns is what they're using to commit violence. Violence is the central problem."*

Wow! What a genius. Rubio figured out that shooting an innocent person is an act of violence. Let's take it back, he *should* be President. So, what is Rubio going to do about violence? After thousands of years of civilization (according to Rubio life on earth began just six thousand years ago), how do we rid society of violence? And does he have any idea of just when that will be accomplished? Does he have a date? But, in the meantime, according to Rubio and others, we should just allow *any* violent person to purchase weapons. Huh?

Where do we get these politicians from? Might they be those *Plutonians?* How can learned people say such crazy things? And how can their words possibly seep through into the minds of their constituents or national followers? But they do. They very easily do. And they go unchallenged. And yet, these words… these *remarkable* words… spoken by these three elected Senators were actually *unremarkable,* extremely *unremarkable*… that is, compared to the words of the next Senator- one of the sponsors of the Manchin-Toomey Bill.

Republican Senator Pat Toomey of Pennsylvania showed himself to be quite brave to co-sponsor this legislation. Not only is Pennsylvania a state with large rural areas where opposition to gun control is as extreme as it gets, but partnering with the other side (the Democrats) on *any* sort of bill is potential political suicide. Therefore, Toomey has to be commended. However, what he said as to why his bill went down to defeat were truly the most remarkable words spoken about the current legislative process and the current Republican Party… And they weren't *crazy* words. It wasn't *intentional nonsense.* Nor were the words a *revelation.* Everyone with an active brainwave already knew what he said was true. But the fact that he actually said it... that a Republican would actually come out and utter the truth in this manner... was *extraordinary*. Here's how Toomey explained to the American people why his bill didn't get enough votes to pass (again, it needed 60 out of 100, instead of just 50):

> *"In the end it didn't pass, because we're so politicized. There were some on my side who did not want to be seen helping the President do something he wanted to get done... just because the President wanted to do it."*

Holy Cow! What is Toomey saying here? What exactly is he saying? Yes, it's obvious... but it's still hard to believe he would actually say this... that these words would actually come from his mouth. Was he given some truth serum?

Toomey is clearly stating that the Republicans would rather see people get shot and killed than have the President accomplish something, or agree with the President on anything- anything!- even if it means saving lives, even if it means going along with what 91% of what the American people would like to see. A Democrat didn't say it. Michael Moore didn't say it. Keith Olbermann didn't say it. Wolf Blitzer didn't say it. Oprah didn't say it. Bill Maher didn't say it. A Republican said it!... You have to be really asleep to hear this statement and not feel somewhat sick inside.

It's not surprising at all to see the entire Republican Party (except for Toomey in this case) work in tandem with LaPierre and the NRA. They seem to be as close as cousins. Even after LaPierre loses his mind and goes off with his *"hellish world"* comments, practically screaming like a child, *"You all just want to see only bad people have guns, so they can kill us all,"* the party still plays a two-headed game with the NRA. Their tactics usually work. And it causes any effort for further gun control to lose steam. They set up proxy arguments, such as claiming that gun owner's rights are being *"chipped away at"*- the so-called "slippery slope" argument- meaning once we let you eliminate one right, you'll then go after more. They both claim that. Funny how you never hear that when the GOP tries chipping away at people's rights –e.g. birth control, abortion, gays and lesbians, unions, patients, voters, etc. You also don't hear them admit when they go against the people's will (91%), even though they routinely accuse the other side of doing so.

Hypocrisy aside, delusion is what usually triumphs, and at the 2013 NRA convention, the Republican Party and the NRA were in a wild celebratory mood due to their defeat- if you want to call it that- of the Manchin-Toomey bill. Several leading Republican figures, including a few who are likely to run for President, addressed the joyous crowd and boasted as if they had just won the *World Series*. However, it was sort of strange. They all seemed oblivious to the fact that they weren't the only ones celebrating. Criminals and those who are dangerously mentally ill were also celebrating the bill's defeat. They were celebrating that they could still very easily get their hands on guns and assault weapons. (It would have been interesting if they had thrown themselves a party next door.)

* * * * *

---

*It's important to note that not *all* NRA members are in line with the leadership of the NRA or the Republican Party. Many- sometimes the majority- are on the complete opposite page. Those who attend the convention are mostly the true *die-hards*. They will cheer any sentence that comes out of each speaker's mouth, no matter how ridiculous or how much opposed it might be by most Americans. It's been thought that if someone with deep pockets was to come along and challenge the NRA with as decent a structure and resources, a large number of members might very well jump ship.

By now, it must seem pretty daunting when you look at what the pro-gun control side is up against. It must seem like an impenetrable wall of nonsense (and callousness). Not to worry. It may be a *thick* wall, but it's not impenetrable. Fortunately, for America (and for the rest of the world, since we sometimes get visitors), the voices mentioned so far are not the only ones we hear out there speaking their minds on gun control. Thankfully, there are others.

It was mentioned earlier what may have been possibly the dumbest conversation on gun control ever- a leader of one of the gun groups suggesting how safe it would be if everyone in a 10,000 seat venue was armed while the President was giving a speech. He also wanted to see passengers be allowed to carry guns on airplanes. Let's now take a galactic leap to the opposite side of this- to what is often called *sanity*- an interview that *CNN's* Anderson Cooper had with Chief Edward Flynn, of the Milwaukee, Wisconsin police department.

The day before this interview, Chief Flynn testified in front of Congress on gun control and gained notoriety because of a heated debate he had with Senator Lindsay Graham (R- South Carolina). Senator Graham made a very common challenge to Chief Flynn- asking him why should there be background checks when criminals who fail the checks are not being prosecuted for lying on the forms. This point is frequently brought up time and again as a way of avoiding an honest discussion. Senator Graham knows full well why these former criminals aren't being prosecuted and he also knows how meaningless this argument is. However, he also knows that most gun owners either aren't aware of, or simply don't understand, the reasons for there being very few prosecutions. And even if they did, he knows they would still be in favor of him carrying out his dishonest charade anyway. When he tried to get it by Chief Flynn, he quickly found out he was up against the wrong person. Chief Flynn would not let him get away with it. He stood his ground and pointed out that it's a *"phony issue"* and a *"red herring"* argument. He knew that Graham knew better and was just playing his usual game of fooling as many people as he could.

Chief Flynn pointed out that background checks have eliminated 76,000 unqualified people from purchasing guns over the past year alone. (Over the course of the last ten years, over 700,000 applications have been denied.) Therefore, background checks *are* doing what they are supposed to do. And they would be doing even more if they were expanded to gun shows and private sales. This would eliminate way more sales of guns to the *wrong people*. Chief Flynn then went on to point out (to the nation) the reality as to why there are so few of these bad applicants being held accountable: He explained that prosecuting people who lie on their application is something that just isn't possible- due to the simple fact that the justice system is already working at *"maximum capacity"* prosecuting murder cases, robberies, assaults, domestic violence, rape, RICO cases, etc. The country's resources are *finite* and it does not have the proper manpower to prosecute a crime that is already being prevented, since, once again, the checks *are* doing the job!

He expanded upon this more the next day in his interview with Anderson Cooper.

Cooper: *"One of the things the NRA says, the logic of something I don't quite understand… is that further background checks at gun shows or private sales would prevent legitimate citizens, upstanding citizens… it would be an inconvenience for them and it's not going to prevent criminals… How would you know, if you're not going to check?"*

Chief Flynn: *"Listen, any working cop will tell you that an awful lot of upstanding citizens are first offenders with a firearm."* And then, drawing an analogy to another massacre, *"What did we determine on 9/11? We as a society would never again allow airplanes to be used as weapons of mass murder. We made a societal-wide commitment and we have inconvenienced the lives of millions of travelers in the laudable social compact that we were going to protect ourselves from airliners being weapons of mass murder. Now, why on earth can we not generate the same will when it comes to military assault weapons and high capacity magazines? We have a slow motion mass murder in this country every year. It's our homicide statistics! And then we have our horrific tragedies as in Aurora and Newtown that should shock the conscience of any responsible public official."* He added: *"Yesterday at the hearing, I was appalled at the number of Senators who were so worried about gun owners' rights they couldn't stick around for the testimony of the people from Newtown. I was appalled. How do you call yourself a public servant and cast aside their testimony? It matters. Saving lives matters. And they seemed dis-interested in that construct."*

Hallelujah! Finally, someone talking *outside* the box! Someone finally standing up to these showcasing Senators and accusing them of making up phony issues, knowing their supporters don't have a clue or don't care. As for Senators making up phony issues, that's not surprising- in fact, it's expected- but Senators getting up and leaving before listening to bereaved families… that's a little hard to accept.

This may not be breaking news, but a lot of our politicians are sorry excuses for human beings. Getting up and leaving before the testimony of the Sandy Hook families is beyond rude, beyond immoral. It's almost like a slap in the face. That's like causing a wound on top of a wound. You don't get up and leave just to avoid seeing the truth for yourself, or to avoid seeing what reality *really* looks like. It's hard to accept there are people like this in the United States Congress, but there are. And they are standing in the way of preventing future tragedies. And they are so easily let off the hook by those who say, *"It's just politics."* Does that excuse them from this behavior? There should be no excuse for this. Too bad there isn't a way for more people to see and understand this behavior for what it is- selfish and inhumane. No matter how you slice it, these Senators have some sort of disconnect to humanity.

But what about the rest of those in Congress- the ones who are good and decent? There *are* some. Right? What can they do?

Just a few weeks prior to Chief Flynn's testimony, *former* Congresswoman Gabrielle Giffords also spoke before Congress. Her speech was slow and she did not say many words. It's remarkable that she can even speak at all after being shot in the head at point blank range. What she did say, though, were perhaps the most profound words spoken in front of Congress after the Sandy Hook shooting. She ended her short speech by asking Congress to *"Be bold."* (It would be nice if she could have ordered them to be bold.) Will Congress ever be bold? Will the President ever be bold? Even though the pro-gun control side of the Senate won- but lost- the first round, they're now going to have to stay with it and become bolder than ever. There *are* questions, though: How scared are they of the NRA? Are they completely convinced that the American people are stupid, and will easily be fooled by the NRA into not re-electing them... unless they drop the issue? Is that what they're scared of? It sure looks that way.

Another voice that was heard and attracted a lot of attention after Sandy Hook was that of Piers Morgan, also of *CNN*. Morgan bravely carried on a one man attack against what he thought was the ridiculous amount of guns that exist in America and the weak laws that allow civilians- any civilian- to purchase military-style weapons. Morgan is from Great Britain, where there is hardly any gun violence at all, mostly because most gun ownership- handguns and assault weapons- are not allowed. Even the police do not routinely carry guns in Great Britain, except for certain situations. Night after night Morgan railed against the nonsensical views of the NRA and other gun organizations, plus individuals who were adamantly against even the slightest change to our gun laws. Morgan did a yeoman's job of fighting for common sense and safety, and against arming the masses. So much so, that a petition arose to deport Morgan from the United States and back to Great Britain. On one of his shows, Morgan to his brave credit, even had on the man responsible for starting the petition. The man huffed and puffed and threatened a revolution- *a la* 1776- if the government tried to take his guns away from him or from any other citizen. Others have decried a similar threat. Morgan took on a great challenge of waging battle against America's gun defenders in a way that most others in his position are far too hesitant (or cowardly) to undertake. However, there were a few times when he missed getting some important points across.

On one of his shows, he was interviewing two women while they were at a shooting range practicing with their semi-automatic assault rifles. The women were strong gun enthusiasts and very outspoken about their views on guns for recreation and self-defense. When one of them stated that the reason she needs an assault rifle, instead of a mere gun or shotgun, was in case *several* bad people invaded her home, Morgan had no response to that. What Morgan should have asked the woman was: given the rare possibility of this happening- there isn't even on record, so far, of an American successfully defending themselves in their home with an assault rifle- was she okay with hundreds of others dying (including 1st and 2nd graders) just so long that she could own an assault rifle to protect herself against an event that most likely will never take place. He should have asked her if this wasn't being incredibly selfish on her part, since if *she* is allowed an assault weapon, it is certain that others, including some very dangerous people, will also be able to get their hands on one.

Now, it doesn't matter what her answer would have been. It is clear that this is one of the main issues of the entire gun control debate: the selfishness on the part of many gun owners. Many gun owners hardly even flinch when massacres happen- an elementary school, a movie theater, the mall, a workplace, etc. Instead, their main concern is always preserving their *right* to have an assault weapon, and to make sure that right isn't in danger. Whether it's for defense or recreation- shooting ranges or hunting- these weapons are a luxury. They have no *necessary* use in the everyday world. Maybe in the movies, but not in real life. The perceived right to have these weapons has produced a stubborn perception of entitlement and imagined fear. Mix those two together and you get words and slogans without any depth or true meaning. As already seen, some of the leaders of various gun groups- especially LaPierre- incite such a strong sense of fear, danger and entitlement, that it leads to acts of terror. One woman got so worked up she sent letters tainted with *ricin*- a deadly substance- to President Obama and others who she felt were a threat to her gun ownership. She claimed it was her "God-given right" to own guns- as if God wrote the Constitution. (It's no longer her *legal* right to own guns, since she is no longer "a law abiding citizen.")

Let's face it- some troubled people want to have the power to *kill*. And it's not that they *are* going to kill, they just want the *power* of having the decision. The power, the decision, and the struggle between the two is almost like a compulsion. In a way, it's no different from a lot of other compulsions that most of us have. We're not all anywhere near perfect, but most of us aren't anywhere near troubled to the point of considering killing someone and having a gun right next to us to engage that thought into action. Why can't most *sane* gun owners recognize this? To be locked in a state of closed mindedness, where you can't see that wanting to own certain killing machines (assault weapons) means that others who are not able to control their thoughts or their hatred will also have access to these machines, is nothing but ignorance and/or selfishness. It's usually impossible for people to see that in themselves, but hopefully more and more people will, because America has a much bigger problem with guns then it cares to admit… and this was clearly proven in the wake of the Sandy Hook massacre… and what happened afterwards.

THE "WHAT IF-FERS"

In the wake of the Sandy Hook massacre gun sales exploded. This has become the norm after several of these tragedies. Whenever the perceived threat of gun control rears up guns sales soar as people think they better purchase their firearms before it's too late. But this time it was different. After Sandy Hook, many gun owners actually turned their assault rifles in. The comprehension of this massacre made them feel that these weapons were just plain wrong to own and had no place in a civilized society. These weapons had suddenly become sacrilegious to many people. There were the polls taken in the very first days after the massacre that showed over 70% of NRA members now favored the banning of these weapons. Several Republican politicians also talked about banning them. And yet, what soared the most out of all the firearm sales were exactly these weapons- assault rifles- particularly the AR-15, the one used at Sandy Hook and previous other massacres. This was pretty disturbing. Who would buy these powerful assault rifles while the country was in a state of mourning as a direct result of these weapons? The most dangerous group of all, that's who- the "what if-fers."

The "what if-fers" are a self-explanatory breed of Americans. They are very simple to understand:

"What if I need to, or (worse yet) *what if I want to… someday use these weapons?"*

There are *three* groups of "what if-fers": The *first* group are those who say they need these weapons to protect against *government tyranny*. And yes, it's true, government tyranny can happen. Any government *can* become tyrannical. But most forms of tyrannical behavior, at least in the last few decades, have come only from the side that anti-gun control proponents identify with- the Republican Party! From Richard Nixon continuing the Vietnam War after most of the country was against it to Iran-Contra where Congress voted against arming Nicaraguan rebels and the Republican White House did it anyway to the Iraq War where most people feel we went to war based on trumped up claims of WMDs to the present day where 91% of Americans were in favor of reducing gun violence through universal background checks and Republican politicians said, "No," tyranny has always come from the anti-gun control side. This group will never acknowledge what is obviously clear: Voting against what 91% of the American people want… *that's* government tyranny!

The *second* group claims they need assault weapons to protect and defend themselves from home invasion and possible other situations- like movie theater and mall shootings. We already discussed the huge odds of that happening and for an assault weapon to be the only and/or best way to survive. We also talked about the selfishness that is involved with this choice- since if *you* get to have these weapons, then *others* will also have access to them.

Both these groups aren't as dangerous as the *third* group. They are only dangerous in the fact that they are the enablers of this third group. They allow this third group to have these weapons.

The *third* group of "what if-fers" are the ones who ran out to purchase these weapons after Sandy Hook not for the sake of needing to protect and defend themselves, but for the purpose of what if they one day *want* to use them. This group, taken as a whole, is loaded (bad word choice) with a suitcase full of "what ifs."

"What if I decide I just can't take it anymore?" "What if I finally decide that this world is just too cruel and unkind to me?" "What if I finally decide that this person who has ruined my life... this guy who stole my wife (or girlfriend)... this person who cost me my job... my business... the kid who humiliated me in the 3rd grade (or high school)...?" "What if I finally decide to take revenge against the Los Angeles police department... and everyone who was responsible for getting me kicked off the force?" "What if I decide to take revenge on the bank that threw me out of my home?" "What if I decide to take revenge on the whole entire world... that seems so happy? Why was I left out?"

And, of course, there are a lot more- including the ever-popular, *"What if I just want to shock the world?"* Or, *"What if I decide I don't like these people... and they deserve to die?"*

This is scary stuff. And it's one of America's dirty little secrets. The country doesn't want to think of this... but it must. It has to. Even

Wayne LaPierre is able to see this. This is where we can all at least *partially* agree with LaPierre when he says:

> *"The truth is that our society is populated by an unknown number of genuine monsters- people so deranged, so evil, so possessed by voices and driven by demons that no sane person can possibly ever comprehend them... Does anybody really believe that the next Adam Lanza isn't planning his attack on a school he's already identified at this very moment?"*

Now, this may have been a case of *projection* on LaPierre's part... but as he was trying to pin the blame solely on the mentally ill, LaPierre intentionally left out, as he usually does (probably because they're good customers), other seriously dangerous groups- angry spouses, angry partners, angry workers, desperate criminals, bank robbers, terrorists, drug traffickers and a brand new group- the *very bored*. Seriously... the very bored. This is no joke. A 22-year-old Australian transfer student attending a small college in Oklahoma on a baseball scholarship was out jogging on a beautiful day when three male teenagers- 15, 16, and 17-years-old- drove up behind him and shot him dead. What was their motive? Why'd they do it? They were *bored*. Once again, this is no joke. They said they were bored and had nothing to do. Whether that's true or not, it's no longer shocking. Pretty unbelievable, isn't it? Australians are now reluctant to visit us. Can you blame them? Anyway, these groups all need to be included in LaPierre's semi-accurate tirade. We just have to do the including *for* him. That's no problem.

This is all very serious- and something to worry about- especially since we know that dozens, hundreds, maybe even thousands of gun sales that took place after Sandy Hook were not made just for safety and defense, or recreation. They were made by individuals who purchased them "just in case"- just in case they would one day not have to, but instead, *want* to use them. As a matter of fact, *gun shows* reported record sales after Sandy Hook. These shows are usually held in large convention halls or event centers. News videos would show them packed to the rafters. Some experts even reported that for the first time gun shows were outselling *gun stores*. What this meant is that many of those who ran out to get these weapons most likely would not have passed a background check. What are we going to do about these people- besides wait until the next tragedy to see just who they are? What can we do? Are there any solutions?

HECK, YEAH!

"Solutions" is an extremely dirty word to those opposed to gun control- especially those who make a living off the sale of guns. Especially the manufacturers. And since there are usually never major changes to gun laws, even after horrible massacres, many in the country have come to accept there *are* no solutions. That's a myth! That there are no solutions… is a myth!

Some solutions to gun violence were mentioned earlier in the first part of the book- stronger and stiffer penalties for possessing an illegal weapon (much stronger), a "war on illegal weapons," eliminating the manufacturing of specific weapons (civilian assault weapons), limiting the manufacturing of the overall number of weapons (which will lower trafficking and stealing), harsher penalties regarding gun responsibility (lock and safe keep and reporting guns missing or stolen right away), gun amnesty and buy-back programs (Los Angeles had one at the end of 2012 and around 1800 weapons were turned in, including 2 surface-to-air missiles), trigger locks, tighter limits on the amount of guns purchased by individuals, plus the three key solutions that have been greatly discussed so far- background checks, assault weapons ban, and magazine limits.

There also needs to be better mental health tracking. All *red flags* have to be *efficiently* documented and investigated. And it should be better known and advertised that if you're feeling stress or other mental discomfort there are resources that you're encouraged to use. The United States needs to greatly expand its treatment for people with mental illness. Plus, mental illness needs to be de-stigmatized so people can get treatment and families don't have to be in denial.

Another solution that can make the streets much safer is also for law enforcement agencies to advertise and make it better known that there are rewards offered for information about illegal guns. (The police offer rewards for information about most crimes. Illegal guns is one of them.) What'll happen is that when one gang's weapons are confiscated, they'll assume it was because of a tip from a rival gang. They will then have to do the same to the rival gang. Then they'll have to go back to the old fashioned way of fighting- hand to hand- until they realize, *"This sucks!"* And then they'll make peace. Guns not only make gang members feel incredibly empowered, but others also. Let's face it, Mickey Mouse can feel like Superman with a gun in his hand.

What also was mentioned were *Gun Checkpoints*. Given the overall gun epidemic that exists today, gun checkpoints can be a very productive way to recover weapons that otherwise may end up being used to commit serious harm and murder. This will undoubtedly be controversial due to existing search and seizure laws- as well as many Americans being in strong denial that gun violence has gone this far. Many will naturally object that "it has come to this"- a random searching of cars. Many of the same people, however, *are* okay with every school in America becoming an armed fortress. *That's* okay for them. That "it has come to that," is okay for them. (The denial factor, as we all know, is complicated and has to do with prejudices involving race, ethnicity, class and politics.)

A gun checkpoint will be similar to a *sobriety* checkpoint. A sobriety checkpoint is something that people in cars, at least the driver, *cannot* avoid. They are rare, but effective, in at least eliminating *some* drivers from causing harm or death. They are also fair. They do not profile or discriminate. You cannot skip or avoid a sobriety checkpoint unless you want to go to jail. Gun checkpoints will be somewhat of a cross between sobriety checkpoints and the *"stop and frisk"* procedure that exists in places like New York City.

However, "stop and frisk" will *always* attract claims of profiling. Gun checkpoints will *not* profile, nor discriminate. During a gun checkpoint, everyone is given the option of turning in whatever illegal firearms they may have in the car- *No Questions Asked*. However, if they don't and a weapon is found, then the penalty is harsh. Very harsh.

One of the possible shortcomings with this could be that if a criminal feels trapped in a bad situation, they may possibly decide to shoot their way out. However, most likely everyone will be aware that no questions are asked, so it's possible this may never happen. That may not stop a paranoid criminal from thinking they might be recognized, but it's also no different from when an armed paranoid criminal gets stopped by the Highway Patrol or Police for a traffic violation. This may need some fine tuning, but nonetheless, this could be a way of getting several illegal guns off the streets- including illegal guns from owners who may be too lazy to go down and participate in a gun amnesty program.

And then there is the last solution- which may possibly be the *best* solution of all. It's an idea conceived by a 7-year-old boy, named Myles. Myles wrote down his idea and sent it off to President Obama, Vice President Biden, and his local representative. The latter two responded. (Now we know what Biden's job is. He answers the mail.) Myles idea is to make the world a safer place by replacing all real bullets with *chocolate* bullets. Just think how great that would be. Someone goes bursting into a movie theater (or church) and starts firing away. Everyone recognizes that the person is upset and has problems. Yet, no one gets hurt. Not only does no one get hurt, but since the chocolates are covered in wrappers, they can easily be picked up off the ground and eaten. Everyone wins. The angry or crazy shooter will have his problems dealt with and some will get a tasty treat. Myles is obviously light years ahead of our lawmakers.

* * * * *

HOORAY?... FOR HOLLYWOOD?

In a book such as this, it may not be legally imperative, but it's probably morally imperative to address the issue of what affect Hollywood entertainment and the video games industry has on gun violence- in fact, all violence- in America. Some say it has plenty of affect and some say it has none. It seems we have not yet reached the point where science can definitively establish which side is correct, even though we sometimes come across a study showing one answer or another. So, therefore, if Hollywood makes a movie or a video company creates a game that shows a killer walking into a school, church, movie theater, etc., and starts firing away at everyone, and then a real life person goes out and copies it, does Hollywood or the video game maker bear any responsibility? The answer is *yes*, but what are you going to do about it? Seriously, what are you going to do about it? Perhaps someone should approach the studios and game makers and ask them in a nice way- a very nice way- to stop making their billions of dollars and to please think about the consequences. (They're good people. They'll most likely forfeit the billions they are making.)

Plus, it's not just the acts of violence that may come from their audience or users. What about the de-sensitization and the de-elevating of millions of minds? How many are being dumbed-down or confused by these extremely violent *fake realities* that many find more appealing to them than their everyday lives? Some may even get lost inside these fantasies- and then what? If only the movies and games were the opposite of these dark fantasies and somehow just as profitable. If only Hollywood could make exciting movies about sewing. There would be more clothes for everyone and less violence.

All kidding aside, it's strange that in a country with so many political and cultural pressure groups, that so little pressure is put on the entertainment industry. The industry is free to make as much money as it likes and also free to express its entertainment any way it likes within the rules of the rating system- but when killer after killer is one of their frequent users, the questions are: Do they care? Are they missing the guilt gene? Or is the profit gene just way too overwhelming?

And again, let's give LaPierre some credit on this one, too. This is exactly how he feels. Except that, with LaPierre, you never know if it's genuine, or if it could be another distraction to get the criticism off of guns. It's not like the NRA- with all their money, power, and influence- follows up with this theory. Instead, this theory just sort of languishes, like *climate change*. You can look out your window any day and see the smoke going up into the air, whether from factories or car engines, and assume for certain that it can't be a good thing. The same with the targeted audience (male *homo sapiens*) of most Hollywood movies and video games featuring guns, explosions, decapitations, assaults, hostage taking, supernatural powers and what not, and also assume for certain that this too can't be a good thing, especially for those who already struggle with reality. It's only the people who like to argue against anything and everything who will say there is no *provable* difference between those who watch a lot of violent movies or play a lot of violent video games and those who do not. The people who work or benefit from these industries will also say the same thing. There are only two things a society can do: either boycott the makers of the entertainment or ask them in a nice way to stop.

But enough about Hollywood and the makers of *Grand Theft Auto* and *Call of Duty* and *Bulletstorm* and *Thrill Kill* and *Splatterhouse* ... the real question is:

WHERE ARE WE HEADED?

(Or, worse yet) WHO'S NEXT?

Since Sandy Hook, gun violence has remained on a steady course. There have been several incidents that gained national attention. Two of the incidents, especially, became highly notable. One was non-shooting and in the second one there was shooting. In the non-shooting incident (a few shots were fired, but no one got hit), it could have possibly been another Sandy Hook. A disturbed young man, who had not been taking his medication, gained entry to a Georgia elementary school with 500 rounds of ammunition. It's not exactly clear if he was determined to shoot children or just get into a shootout with the police. (He apparently had a grudge against the police.) Luckily, an incredibly brave employee of the school was able to talk him down- it was all caught on a 911 recording- and he surrendered without hurting anyone.

The second incident was at the Washington, D.C. Navy Yard. A disgruntled contractor who worked there shot and killed 12 people. No one as of yet knows exactly why. He apparently had some acute mental or emotional issues, but supposedly, he was upset with his employer and his action took some planning. So, was it anger, mental illness, or both? No one may ever know, since the shooter was shot dead by a police officer. Nonetheless, he had legally purchased a high-powered shotgun just a few days prior to carrying out his act, even though he had past episodes with guns and was discharged from the Navy after several incidents of misconduct. But since it was an honorable discharge, it kept him eligible to purchase weapons- which seems wrong, but not surprising.

The fact that none of the victims (except for one of the guards) were armed, nor were any of the other workers (only the guards on the base are allowed to carry weapons), brought up a very common point that is often raised by the anti-gun control crowd:

"If the people who worked there were armed, then they might have been able to stop him."

Here's why you can't have people armed in most workplaces:

Because workplaces are environments where there is often a lot of *tension*.

Even though workplace shootings occur, human nature most often works in a way so that when there's a conflict between co-workers or with a boss, a cooling off period… usually *cools things off.* If someone is armed, they might react in the moment… the moment when they are *out of control.*

Just imagine the atmosphere if some or all employees are carrying a gun: *"Hey, better be nice to Tom in receiving and give him what he wants. He gets awful angry… and explosive."*

How are people supposed to work when they're scared for their lives???? And knowing, or thinking that someone has a gun changes things and adds an element of fear to almost *every* situation.

It's extremely difficult to stop workplace shootings, or keep people from "going postal." Fortunately, they are rare- although, each one is too many. It would be nice if the Human Resources Department of most companies were more efficient and got a better handle on the stresses that exist. But just think how many angry episodes there have been where someone later thought, *"Good thing I didn't have a gun in my hand…"* and instead they had time to think it through.

And thinking it through would probably be the best way for all of America to go on the entire issue of guns. Instead, it's not being thought through. The clowns are doing the thinking for the ones who can't think and the lobbyists are pulling the strings for the ones who think only of themselves. And so, we're headed nowhere. We just stand still and wait for the next shooting to occur.

Even though America may very well one day pass stronger gun control legislation, it's possible that things will get a lot worse and more mass shootings will take place before that happens. You have to wonder, when will the moment come when the country finally says (and means), *"Enough"*? A lot of people first thought Columbine was that moment, and then other tragedies, and then, of course, people thought for sure that Sandy Hook was that moment. It would sure be nice if all the pain and heartache can be spared or bypassed and we can just skip right to it, but that may be too much wishful thinking on the part of most Americans.

America has fallen into a sorrowful pit of inertia over the gun issue (thank you, Congress), where the argument is in a collapsed state between *common sense* and *nonsense*. And if you're on the side of the 91% who thinks there ought to be some scrutiny for anyone who wants to purchase a gun, then you're on the side of common sense. The same holds true for those on the side of the civilian ban on assault weapons and the limit on high capacity magazines. But, even though most Americans may be on the side of common sense, what good is that going to do for the next victim or victims? What good is that going to do if you're the next victim or a loved one is the next victim?

The side that is feeding and preserving the nonsense is formidable- there's no doubt about that. But the way that our government is *supposed* to work- they're only as formidable in this instance as politicians on the other side are weak, or "the people" lose hope. It's unfortunate, but that's how it goes. (Maybe we should have some pity for the politician and the gun industry's dilemma of being responsible and doing what's best for society as opposed to making the highest possible profits for themselves and their shareholders. What a lousy excuse they live with!)

After Sandy Hook, President Obama finally promised to enact changes that were within his power. He made this promise while standing in front of the people of Newtown, Connecticut just a few days after the massacre. Sadly, and apparently, he has little power to do anything when it comes to guns- even though it's puzzling that this isn't considered a national emergency. If a foreign country or terrorist attacked and killed a tiny fraction of the number of Americans that are killed each year by firearms... *that* would be a national emergency. Maybe it's the President's fault, and maybe it isn't. But having 91% of the country on your side and not being able to fix something this serious, even though you're the President, has got to mean there's a problem with the definition of government. The

President is not a dictator, that's true… but neither is the Republican Party… or the NRA.

What's been going on for the last few decades is that the side that wants stronger gun control laws has been playing *softball* against a team that has been playing *hardball*. And therefore it's been left up to "the people" who are connected to common sense and who truly care about the health, safety, and well-being of others to stay strong and engaged and support all the victims and their families. It's not easy. Unfortunately, Sandy Hook happened at a really bad time, shortly after a national election- meaning that 2 years will have had to go by until the next national election for the country to change things through the ballot box. A lot of other important, as well as, contrived issues are going to pop up in the meantime. And a lot of people are going to forget Sandy Hook and other past shootings as they go back to their daily lives of trying not to think about these sad events. Some might even get fooled once again by the lies of the NRA and various politicians into thinking that their nonsense does indeed make sense. The NRA, politicians, and other corrupt voices are very good at that. As mentioned earlier, even in May of 2013, the most popular radio voice in the nation wanted his audience to believe that the country was overwhelmingly *against* background checks and other forms of gun control. Seriously, despite what all legitimate polls revealed, he wanted his audience to believe otherwise. And you just have to wonder… what actually goes through his listeners' minds? Do they just automatically accept this? Do they automatically agree with him? Does it change their minds just in case they reasonably thought otherwise based on their *own* observations? You just have to wonder. You just really have to wonder. What kind of information are some people being fed?

The only answer may be, for those in favor of gun control, is to gain more courage and stand up to the lies and crazy arguments that come from the gun lobby. Stand up to your crazy brother or father-in-law or cousin or friend. Refute what they have to say, even though it might not be part of your character or personality. Lives are at stake. It won't be easy. That's for sure. For instance, you can go to any town hall meeting and there can be 100 people there who are in favor of stronger gun control and only 10 people *screaming* against it. Usually, those 10 screaming against gun control will easily *out-shout* those 100 who are in favor of stricter controls. The intensity level is no where near evenly matched. The minority who are against gun control for whatever crazy reasons are always going to be intimidating to people who have witnessed their rage, their lack of sensitivity, and their stubborn refusal to reach a fair and democratic resolution to gun ownership, gun availability, and gun violence. It's only natural that many do not want to engage in a fight over this. But every little bit that someone does to reverse the nonsense and insanity of having little or no gun control- and keeps it going until the next election- will be making a valuable effort towards possibly saving a person's life. Sometime it's a lot of persons. It could even be another classroom full of children.

APPENDIX A

HOW TO ARGUE GUN CONTROL

It's hard to win an argument when you're arguing against an opponent who you may want to describe as stubborn, narrow-minded, disagreeable, or someone determined not to let anything you say convince them that the earth might be round. Even some very well paid and successful voices frequently say the most moronic things about gun control. Statements like: *"Why don't we outlaw cars? Cars kill people."* Or, *"Why don't we get rid of knives? People use knives to kill."* After the Boston Marathon bombing… *"Now they're going to want to outlaw pressure cookers* (used by the bombers) *and nails* (placed inside the bombs). *How are we going to build homes… or cook rice?"* Plus, as mentioned in the book, the intensity level when arguing gun control is way unevenly matched. Some gun owners, we've all seen, can get pretty surly and aggressive. Let's face it, someone saying, *"You come for my guns* (even though no one is coming for their guns) *and I'll kill ya,"* usually comes off sounding far more aggressive than someone pleading, *"Can you please be reasonable?"*

Let's just say it! No one side usually has a monopoly on what is common sense… *except* for this one issue regarding guns! Even semi-intelligent gun owners know, at a minimum, that it's beyond logic to allow certain people to purchase weapons. And that if you don't check people out first to see if they have a history of crime or mental illness, then you're putting the public at great risk.

Most people who argue against reasonable gun control are often consumed by NRA or right-wing *talking points*, since that's all they ever listen to. Arguing against brainwashed or narrow-minded people is not easy. However, there is always the hope that you can wake them up. They are never going to be de-programmed unless someone gives it a try.

Therefore, if and when you find yourself in a situation where you're up against these *talking points* and you want to express your desire for a society with less guns, zero assault weapons, and as strong an effort as possible to keep guns out of the wrong hands, here are some brief arguments you may want to use:

UNIVERSAL BACKGROUND CHECKS

PRO-GUN CONTROL: A person convicted of a felony, or a certain type of misdemeanor, or a person deemed mentally ill, should not be allowed to purchase a firearm in any case whatsoever.

ANTI-GUN CONTROL: We agree, but background checks don't work.

PRO: Background checks work. The *National Instant Criminal Background Check System-* NICS- has denied over 700,000 applications out of more than 100 million requests over the last 10 years. That's over 700,000 applicants who tried to purchase a firearm and were denied. If gun shows, private sellers, and the internet required background checks, the number of applicants denied would be way more. And just how many of those guns that were denied, would have ended up being used for a crime? And just how many guns purchased at gun shows, or from private sellers, or over the internet that would have been denied had there been a background check... how many of *those* guns *were* used for a crime?

Plus... you say you agree that you want to keep felons and those who are mentally ill from purchasing a firearm, yet you want to leave the system exactly the way it is, meaning that *anyone* (who looks of age) can purchase a firearm legally without a background check (except in states with tougher laws than federal). This makes no sense.

ANTI: A criminal is not going to submit to a background check. You'll only be inconveniencing law abiding citizens.

PRO: First of all, some criminals do submit an application. That's the main reason for the rejections. They either lie on the form or they hope that it sneaks through. (Some may not understand they are not qualified.) With universal background checks, if they *don't* submit to a background check, then they can't purchase a firearm- *legally*. There's no place for them to legally go. That leaves only 3 ways for them to get a firearm- steal one, get someone to buy one for them (*a straw purchase*), or purchase one from a gun *trafficker*. Each one is not anywhere near as easy as people like to think. Do you really think that if Adam Lanza walked into a rough and tumble neighborhood and inquired about where to get a gun he would have walked out of that neighborhood with a firearm, let alone the money he came with? *Indiana Jones* might even return home in his underwear from some parts of town. And if *stealing* was so easy, it would be a sport! And getting someone (*a straw purchaser*) to risk being liable when you commit your crime… good luck with that.

And second… you have to be kidding. Inconvenience law abiding citizens???? Law abiding citizens have to practically get naked before boarding an airplane! We have to take out all metal objects before entering certain buildings and public events. Life is *constantly* inconvenient! There are traffic jams. Friends always late. Lines at the supermarket. The DMV- for God's sake. And perhaps the most inconvenient of all- as the daughter of the principal of Sandy Hook Elementary School brought up to Senator Kelly Ayotte (R- New Hampshire), who voted against universal background checks- the inconvenience of burying your mother, spouse, or child. What about that inconvenience? That doesn't count? Who ever would have thought that *"being an inconvenience"* would ever be used as an argument against gun control after all the murders we have seen?

And please, as for *"law abiding citizens"*- a line that's used *ad nauseam*: Not all so-called "law abiding citizens" *are* law abiding. Many have broken several laws- including some horrible offenses- but just haven't gotten caught yet. Plus, many law abiding citizens use a firearm, some fatally, while committing their first offense.

ANTI: Universal Background Checks will lead to a universal gun registry. Creating a registry is a step towards taking away our guns. The 2nd Amendment protects us against government tyranny.

PRO: The *Manchin-Toomey Bill* addressed the issue of a gun registry, making it a mandatory 15 year prison sentence for anyone who establishes one. Unless a state passes a law requiring registration and/or permits, no registry is legally allowed to be established.

But here's the real absurdity of this: Do you know who actually does have a gun registry? The NRA. Yes, that's right. The NRA! Their defense is that they do it for marketing purposes. It just seems pretty hypocritical of the NRA and gun owners when they say they don't want the government to have a registry, because the day the government becomes tyrannical and wants to take everyone's gun away, the army will know exactly where to go. However, the rest of the population, apparently, isn't supposed to be concerned when an angry and threatening NRA wants to go to war if they ever don't get their way. And they know exactly where every gun owner and crazy militia leader is located, and can mobilize them in an instant! Why is one different than the other?

The majority of Americans are overwhelmingly in favor of a gun registry so that law enforcement can solve crimes and get violent criminals off the street. And when this is very simply explained to the public, the numbers go up even higher. However, there are still some who think the United States is one day going to become an evil dictatorship or the United Nations is going to lead a *One World* government with countries like Israel and Iran or Pakistan and India holding hands and singing *Kumbaya* together. In that case there has to be an island lying somewhere in one of the oceans where they can move to before this happens.

ASSAULT WEAPONS BAN

PRO: These killing machines are designed to kill as many people as possible and as quickly as possible. They do not belong in civilian hands. They belong in the hands of the police and military.

ANTI: We have a right to use whatever we want, whatever means are necessary to defend ourselves. What if my home is broken into by a *gang of thugs*?

PRO: Describe what *means* may be necessary. A machine gun? A missile? Nerve gas? If you're allowed any of these, then others will also be able to get them. A society has to establish a bar concerning risks. A gang of thugs breaking into a home is a rare occurrence, although, it has happened and will happen again. But certain risks or steps taken to protect the greater number of society versus protecting the very few is how most societies roll. There is always some sacrifice and some risk for the greater good.

It's perfectly okay that some people are built *without* the "sacrifice" gene. They may have a very strong "selfish" or "protective" gene and just care about protecting themselves and their families, no matter what the outcome might be for others. It just seems that with all the long shot reasons for wanting to own powerful weapons, some gun owners sound like they don't even believe in stepping outside their door for fear of a lightning strike.

ANTI: I don't want an assault weapon for self-defense. I want it for recreational use- target shooting and hunting.

PRO: That might be acceptable to most people... as long as it's kept locked up (along with the ammunition) at the shooting ranges. Many people leave their valuables in a safe deposit box and their work clothes in a locker. Kids keep stuff in their lockers at school. And you lock up your jewelry... and your guns... hopefully.

As for hunting with an assault rifle... most outdoorsmen feel that's overkill and unethical. For those who insist on hunting this way (and if it's legal), the rifles can be checked out from a safe place and then returned.

MAGAZINE LIMITS- 10 ROUNDS

(This sort of overlaps with assault weapons, because some people feel that if you limit the magazine capacity then, therefore, the assault weapons aren't as lethal, so why ban them? However, a skilled gunman *can* change magazines very quickly, canceling out the effect. Plus, most likely a *black market* will emerge specifically for high capacity magazines.)

ANTI: It's useless. It takes seconds to change magazines.

PRO: Not *all* murderous shooters are experts. Having to change a magazine gives the target (*or targets*) a chance to escape, or to fight back against the shooter. 11 children were able to escape when the Sandy Hook shooter had to change magazines. And Gabrielle Gifford's assailant was tackled by a 63-year-old woman and captured while he also had to change magazines.

ANTI: I have a right to defend my home and myself. What if it takes more than 10 bullets?

PRO: Does it upset you when someone fires dozens or even hundreds of bullets into a crowd in a matter of seconds, killing several people?

Have you ever heard of someone firing that many bullets to defend themselves?

THE SECOND AMENDMENT

ANTI: The 2nd Amendment establishes my God-given right to own a gun. It is *inviolate*. The 2nd Amendment is what makes it possible for all my other rights to exist. The 2nd Amendment allows me, a law abiding citizen, the right to defend myself with a gun against non-law abiding citizens. The Supreme Court, in *District of Columbia v. Heller*, has ruled that I indeed, as an individual, and not a member of a militia, have the right to own firearms.

PRO: The 2nd Amendment is the only amendment in the Constitution that refers to a piece of machinery- a 1776 style pistol and a 1776 style rifle- a.k.a. musket. The Founding Fathers had no idea that guns would ever be as powerful as they are today. And when ruling against a key provision in the 1965 Voters Rights Act, Supreme Court Chief Justice John Roberts claimed that since things are different now than they were back in 1965, some laws need to be changed. Hmm. Weren't things different some two and a half centuries ago when a musket fired one single shot… and it took almost a minute to reload? Plus, as the hero of judicial conservatism, Supreme Court Justice Antonin Scalia ruled in the *Heller* case, the 2nd Amendment does not prohibit *limitations*- something that Scalia may have regretted when the NRA took down his statue and scratched him off their Christmas list.

The following *slogan*, and then *talking point*, are almost guaranteed to come up when arguing gun control:

"Guns don't kill people. People do!"

This is probably the most effective slogan that the gun lobby has ever come up with. It's their *all-star* slogan- just a few simple words that dumbfound the opposing side and makes it tough to argue with. Very few people know how to respond when they hear this. It's even produced a silly offspring… that goes something like this:

"These gun control nuts must actually think that an alarm clock goes off in the morning, the gun gets out of bed, takes its shower, has its coffee, makes a few phone calls, and then goes out and starts shooting people. That's what they think!... Guns don't do this! People do this!"

Okay. *We getcha.* It's amazing for us to have to say this, but… NO ONE THINKS THIS!!!!

This is why the lack of critical thinking on the part of so many Americans is dangerous. No one who is for stronger gun control is saying that a gun gets out of bed and walks outside and starts shooting people. We know that guns don't have a mind of their own and that it's people who pick them up and do the shooting. (We learned this in kindergarten.) And we know that just giving the simple response, "Yes, people kill people. But they do it… WITH GUNS," just isn't enough for you. Except… here's the problem:

There is no way of knowing *which people* are going to do the killing!!!!

So, therefore… we want to lessen the odds! We don't understand why you don't want to lessen the odds so that someday it won't be *your* son, daughter, wife, husband, cousin, friend, teacher, neighbor, co-worker… who is the next victim.

It's all about lessening the odds. And since the odds are known to increase for people with histories of crime or mental illness, we want to make sure that it's as difficult as possible for them to get their hands on any type of firearm- especially ones designed to kill the most people in the least amount of time. If they do manage to get a firearm, we at least want the target (or targets) to have a chance.

The bottom line is: We CAN control guns, but we CAN'T control people's behavior.

"If everyone is armed, no one will mess with ya."

Not true. And it goes contrary to what anti-gun control people always say: *"If a bad person is determined to cause harm… they will find a way."* If that's true, then they will *still* find a way- a more aggressive way.

If everyone is thought to be armed, then, very likely, a bad person won't walk up to someone and point a gun at them, they'll walk up to someone and immediately start shooting- or shoot them from behind. And if they're caught- and the victim *was* armed- they'll claim self-defense, or in some states, *Stand Your Ground* (see Appendix B).

And what about the more vulnerable in our society- (some) seniors, (some) women, children, and the handicapped… or anyone who just might not be quick enough on the draw?

When Larry Pratt, Executive Director of the *Gun Owners of America*, was asked if he's against *all* background checks, which, in that case, would make it even easier for criminals and disturbed people to buy guns, his answer was yes- just as long as the government doesn't take his guns away from him. So, just because *he* feels safe and competent enough to protect himself if *everyone* had guns, that's good enough for him, and the way it should be.

Just imagine a fully armed or almost-fully armed society. How are Mr. or Mrs. Smith- who are 90 years old and maybe not as sharp as they once were- how are they going to exist or survive in this *Wild West* society? Are they just supposed to bolt their doors and never come out? And criminals, being aware that almost everyone has a gun, will target the vulnerable like never before knowing there's something extremely valuable and useful for them to steal- their gun! So, for the very few (and there are few, otherwise you would be reading about them daily) and far in between successful *defenses* involving guns, out of the thousands of successful *assaults*, is that what's considered a great plan? This doesn't make sense or seem fair.

And last... perhaps the two most challenging questions for either side:

Question one (to a person in favor of stronger gun control)-

"If someone had a gun pointed at you or was shooting at you or your loved ones (or even at others)...wouldn't you wish at that moment that you had a firearm in your hands?"

Question two (to a person opposed to stronger gun control)-

"What if someone with a history of criminal activity or a history of being in and out of mental institutions attended a gun show and purchased an assault rifle and a large amount of ammunition without any questions asked, and then a week later walked into a mall and- using a 100 round magazine- began firing away... and murdered your child? How would you feel then about universal background checks, an assault weapons ban, and limiting magazines to 10 rounds? Would you still be against stronger gun control?"

These are difficult questions to answer (for most people). That's for sure. No matter from which side of the aisle you're on, there are no easy answers. And it's not just the *yes, no,* and *perhaps/maybe* part of the response that matters, but the true personal feelings and rationale behind whatever answer one gives.

In the end it comes down to who's being truthful with themselves- and, if you're going to speak out, who's being truthful to others. Most people realize how important this issue is and yet accept feeling defeated by the indifference of politicians- who don't typically live in the real world where there are gangs, drug addicts; and desperate, angry and alienated people- including those suffering from mental illness who are not being treated. We all hate saying it's a dangerous world out there, because we wish that it wasn't. And we all know that there's no stopping *every* criminal, or *every* disturbed person, or *every* person of ill-will, or *every* person who may one day snap from getting a gun... However, we *can* make it more difficult for them to get a gun. But first, we have to vote the politicians who choose *not* to make it more difficult for the wrong people to get guns... out of office!

APPENDIX B

STAND YOUR GROUND

The *Stand Your Ground Law*- which allows for the use of deadly force to defend yourself if you feel that your life or physical safety is in danger- is a huge major threat to gun control. Not many people ever even heard of the law- except for in the two dozen or so states where it already existed- until a Black teenager, Trayvon Martin, was shot and killed in the town of Sanford, Florida. And now that the law has been highlighted and is out in the open, the nature of gun ownership (at least in those states) is likely to evolve… and not in a positive way.

In consideration now is the added difficulty of being able to convict a shooter who claims *Stand Your Ground* as their defense. Plus, due to the fear that this will make future assailants more aggressive, the law is bound to up the ante in gun ownership. In simple terms, non-criminal types (a.k.a. most Americans) will now give further consideration to having a gun on them for safety when they step outside their homes- especially at night.

This is just a terrible all-around law, and people wonder how could state legislatures pass this in the first place? The answer is simple: If the NRA can defeat background checks, they couldn't possibly have had much trouble getting *Stand Your Ground* passed in these several states.

The shooting of Trayvon Martin (a 17 year old Black kid) by George Zimmerman (a White-Hispanic adult) took place in Sanford on February 26, 2012, almost eleven months prior to Sandy Hook. The trial of George Zimmerman, who at first wasn't charged with murder and was given the *Stand Your Ground* benefit of the doubt until national protests pressured law enforcement into taking a closer look, was played out before the eyes of America on a nationally televised stage almost eight months *after* Sandy Hook. It captured the thoughts and imagination of the country in many ways, with gun control being one of them.

Although the trial had to stick to the legal process and couldn't go off in a direction towards gun control (many feel, however, that it did go off in a direction towards *race*), the issue was on many people's minds, simply because Florida is a *Stand Your Ground* state. And although *Stand Your Ground* wasn't used during the trial as part of the defense- possibly because the defense lawyers may have been concerned the law would be ripped to shreds- the verdict of the trial may very well have hinged solely on the law's existence, since the definition of *Stand Your Ground* was read to the jury as part of the jury's instructions. And according to one juror's post-trial statement, indeed that *was* the basis for the not guilty verdict.

Now, this case is definitely going to have repercussions over the issue of gun control, mainly because states that have the *Stand Your Ground* law will naturally have other laws favoring anti-gun control. States with weak gun laws naturally have a higher rate of gun ownership. In fact, it's hard to imagine any gun legislation favored by the NRA and other gun organizations that doesn't lead to higher gun ownership. So, thinking ahead, what could this possibly lead to?

After the tragedy of Sandy Hook, anti-gun control advocates really began to make the push that more people should be armed. They weren't just calling for teachers to be armed and to have armed officers on the campus of all schools, but on the whole, they want more people walking the streets of America armed and loaded as a way (they say) to stop and deter crime. Hence, for now on, every shooting that takes place in a public setting will always be followed by this argument. And for those who have always wondered just how much sense this makes... Well, here's your answer!

The George Zimmerman-Trayvon Martin murder trial proved beyond a shadow of a doubt that a *lamebrain* such as George Zimmerman should indeed not be armed while out in public. This was a textbook case of how dangerous it is for certain people to be allowed to carry a concealed weapon. The overwhelming consensus was that Zimmerman showed an incredible amount of poor judgment and ineptitude in his actions that led to this fatal confrontation. In fact, Zimmerman should probably be the *poster boy* for why no one should be armed while outside their home, except for law enforcement and very few other exceptions.

There is a *reason* why before becoming a police officer, recruits first enter a building called, *The Police Academy*. There's a reason why soldiers who enlist don't go off to war the very next day. There's a reason why you're not allowed to drive in the *Indy 500* the day after you receive your driver's license. There's this very ancient concept called, "training." Serious training. (And not just how to shoot... but also how to deal with all sorts of situations.)

Here is the stupidity of the *Stand Your Ground* law and what the trial's exposure of the law clearly revealed: First, the saying used to go: *"You don't bring a gun (or knife) to a fistfight."* Well, now you do. You can't lose. Once you feel things aren't going your way, you can just shoot the other person- especially if no one is around. And *if* no one is around, it's better to shoot to kill, so he or she can never testify against you.

It's curious that it was never brought up in the trial (maybe it wasn't allowed to), but why didn't Zimmerman just shoot Trayvon in the arm or leg? If Trayvon was on top of Zimmerman, as was believed to be the case, he most likely wouldn't have missed, and Trayvon would have backed off and retreated. Not that Zimmerman was thinking of that at the time, but as it turns out, Zimmerman was fortunate he *didn't* just shoot Trayvon in the arm or leg.

After witnessing this trial and how this tragedy and confrontation was played out, wouldn't the NRA finally agree that guns are without a doubt too dangerous in too many people's hands? Would they now see this as a clear example of how easy it is for things to go wrong? Sure... quit daydreaming.

Here's what a situation like this shows: Imagine if Zimmerman was in the Aurora movie theater on that fateful night when 70 people were shot. You could just easily picture him firing away in the direction of the shooter, but striking innocent person after innocent person. Afterwards, he would have simply claimed that he did what he thought was right. And that's the problem!

A lot of people would easily have said, *"Well, he might have hit the shooter."* No! No! No! You can't have it in individuals' heads that they are crime stoppers or some kind of hero they imagine themselves to be. In 2012 there was a shooting in New York outside the Empire State Building. A man shot and killed his former co-worker. The police chased down the shooter through the crowded streets (it's always crowded there) and fired 16 shots at him, killing him, but also striking nine innocent bystanders. These were trained police officers doing the shooting and they still managed to shoot several bystanders. Do we really want untrained civilians playing cop?

Imagine if there were people around that fatal night when Zimmerman followed Trayvon and provoked their confrontation. Imagine if Trayvon *was* a criminal or if he was mentally ill and he fought with Zimmerman and took his gun away from him and started shooting others. (And apparently Zimmerman's gun *could* be taken away, or so he felt, since that was one of the reasons he gave for why he had to shoot Trayvon.)

So, there's your answer, NRA. You keep using the fact that there are millions of dangerous criminals and people who are mentally ill out there, and it's not safe for anyone who is unarmed. And yet, you want there to be millions of George Zimmermans out there. In that case- who *is* safe?! Is anyone safe?!

This murder and trial and further divisiveness of race issues never would have happened if George Zimmerman didn't have a gun. Instead, besides a 17-year-old kid who was minding his own business being dead, gun sales will surge even further now, especially in the states that have *Stand Your Ground* laws, since everyone now knows that it's okay, maybe even beneficial for them, to now *"bring a gun to a fistfight."*

APPENDIX C

23 INITIATIVES

(PROPOSED BY THE VICE PRESIDENT'S TASK FORCE)

1. Issue a Presidential Memorandum to require federal agencies to make relevant data available to the federal background check system.

2. Address unnecessary legal barriers, particularly relating to the Health Insurance Portability and Accountability Act, that may prevent states from making information available to the background check system.

3. Improve incentives for states to share information with the background check system.

4. Direct the Attorney General to review categories of individuals prohibited from having a gun to make sure dangerous people are not slipping through the cracks.

5. Propose rulemaking to give law enforcement the ability to run a full background check on an individual before returning a seized gun.

6. Publish a letter from ATF to federally licensed gun dealers providing guidance on how to run background checks for private sellers.

7. Launch a national safe and responsible gun ownership campaign.

8. Review safety standards for gun locks and gun safes (Consumer Product Safety Commission).

9. Issue a Presidential Memorandum to require federal law enforcement to trace guns recovered in criminal investigations.

10. Release a DOJ report analyzing information on lost and stolen guns and make it widely available to law enforcement.

11. Nominate an ATF director.

12. Provide law enforcement, first responders, and school officials with proper training for active shooter situations.

13. Maximize enforcement efforts to prevent gun violence and prosecute gun crime.

14. Issue a Presidential Memorandum directing the Centers for Disease Control to research the causes and prevention of gun violence.

15. Direct the Attorney General to issue a report on the availability and most effective use of new gun safety technologies and challenge the private sector to develop innovative technologies.

16. Clarify that the Affordable Care Act does not prohibit doctors asking their patients about guns in their homes.

17. Release a letter to health care providers clarifying that no federal law prohibits them from reporting threats of violence to law enforcement authorities.

18. Provide incentives for schools to hire school resource officers.

19. Develop model emergency response plans for schools, houses of worship and institutions of higher education.

20. Release a letter to state health officials clarifying the scope of mental health services that Medicaid plans must cover.

21. Finalize regulations clarifying essential health benefits and parity requirements within ACA exchanges.

22. Commit to finalizing mental health parity regulations.

23. Launch a national dialogue led by Secretaries Sebelius and Duncan on mental health.

ACKNOWLEDGEMENTS

Special thanks to the cartoonists who contributed their great work to this book: Steven Greenberg, Robert Ariail, Paul Berge, Bruce Plante, and Kate Salley Palmer. Special thanks to the website: *One Million Moms and Dads Against Gun Violence*. Special thanks to Sophie Green for her editing skills. And, of course, special thanks to family and friends who supported this effort.

ABOUT THE AUTHOR

Steve Freeman was born in New York City, attended NYU, read *On the Road*, and took off… on the road. After living most of his life in big cities, he grew tired of the gun violence, narrowly escaping one incident, and moved to Northern California, just outside of Sacramento. He was always interested in the issue of gun control, but after Sandy Hook, he couldn't get the issue or incident off his mind and decided to write a book about the motives of those who want very little or hardly any gun control at all. (And yes, there are some who want no gun control at all, but luckily they are a very small minority. Loud, but small.)

Follow Steve Freeman at-

Website: www.GunsinAmericathebook.com

Facebook: www.facebook.com/GunsInAmericathebook

Twitter: @GunsAmericaBook

Email: GunsinAmericaTwitter@gmail.com

Printed in Great Britain
by Amazon.co.uk, Ltd.,
Marston Gate.